# Physical Modeling in MATLAB®

Allen B. Downey

Version 1.1.1

# Physical Modeling in MATLAB®

Copyright 2008 Allen B. Downey

The original form of this book is LaTeX source code. Compiling this LaTeX source has the effect of generating a device-independent representation of a book, which can be converted to other formats and printed.

This book was typeset by the author using latex, dvips and ps2pdf, among other free, open-source programs. The LaTeX source for this book is available from `http://greenteapress.com/matlab`.

"MATLAB" is a registered trademark of The Mathworks, Inc. The Mathworks does not warrant the accuracy of this book; they probably don't even like it.

ISBN 978-0-6151-8550-7

# Preface

Most books that use MATLAB are aimed at readers who know how to program. This book is for people who have never programmed before.

As a result, the order of presentation is unusual. The book starts with scalar values and works up to vectors and matrices very gradually. This approach is good for beginning programmers, because it is hard to understand composite objects until you understand basic programming semantics. But there are problems:

- The MATLAB documentation is written in terms of matrices, and so are the error messages. To mitigate this problem, the book explains the necessary vocabulary early and deciphers some of the messages that beginners find confusing.

- Many of the examples in the first half of the book are not idiomatic MATLAB. I address this problem in the second half by translating the examples into a more standard style.

The book puts a lot of emphasis on functions, in part because they are an important mechanism for controlling program complexity, and also because they are useful for working with MATLAB tools like `fzero` and `ode45`.

I assume that readers know calculus, differential equations, and physics, but not linear algebra. I explain the math as I go along, but the descriptions might not be enough for someone who hasn't seen the material before.

There are small exercises within each chapter, and a few larger exercises at the end of some chapters.

This is Version 1.0 of the book. I used Version 0.9 for my class in Fall 2007. I made some corrections based on feedback from students and others, then added some exercises and additional chapters. If you have suggestions and corrections, please send them to `downey@allendowney.com`.

Allen B. Downey
Needham, MA
December 28, 2007

## Contributor's list

The following are some of the people who have contributed to this book:

- Michael Lintz spotted the first (of many) typos.

- Kaelyn Stadtmueller reminded me of the importance of linking verbs.

- Roydan Ongie knows a matrix when he sees one.

- Keerthik Omanakuttan knows that acceleration is not the second derivative of acceleration.

- Pietro Peterlongo pointed out that Binet's formula is an exact expression for the $n$th Fibonacci number, not an approximation.

# Contents

**Preface**    i

**1 Variables and values**    1

   1.1   A glorified calculator . . . . . . . . . . . . . . . . . . . . . . . . 1

   1.2   Math functions . . . . . . . . . . . . . . . . . . . . . . . . . . . . 2

   1.3   Documentation . . . . . . . . . . . . . . . . . . . . . . . . . . . . 3

   1.4   Variables . . . . . . . . . . . . . . . . . . . . . . . . . . . . . . . 4

   1.5   Assignment statements . . . . . . . . . . . . . . . . . . . . . . . 5

   1.6   Why variables? . . . . . . . . . . . . . . . . . . . . . . . . . . . 5

   1.7   Errors . . . . . . . . . . . . . . . . . . . . . . . . . . . . . . . . 6

   1.8   Floating-point arithmetic . . . . . . . . . . . . . . . . . . . . . 7

   1.9   Comments . . . . . . . . . . . . . . . . . . . . . . . . . . . . . . 9

   1.10   Glossary . . . . . . . . . . . . . . . . . . . . . . . . . . . . . . . 9

   1.11   Exercises . . . . . . . . . . . . . . . . . . . . . . . . . . . . . . . 10

**2 Scripts**    11

   2.1   M-files . . . . . . . . . . . . . . . . . . . . . . . . . . . . . . . . 11

   2.2   Why scripts? . . . . . . . . . . . . . . . . . . . . . . . . . . . . . 12

   2.3   The workspace . . . . . . . . . . . . . . . . . . . . . . . . . . . . 13

   2.4   More errors . . . . . . . . . . . . . . . . . . . . . . . . . . . . . . 13

   2.5   Pre- and post-conditions . . . . . . . . . . . . . . . . . . . . . . 14

   2.6   Assignment and equality . . . . . . . . . . . . . . . . . . . . . . 15

   2.7   Incremental development . . . . . . . . . . . . . . . . . . . . . . 15

2.8   Unit testing . . . . . . . . . . . . . . . . . . . . . . . . . . . .   16

2.9   Glossary . . . . . . . . . . . . . . . . . . . . . . . . . . . . . .   17

2.10  Exercises  . . . . . . . . . . . . . . . . . . . . . . . . . . . . .   18

## 3   Loops                                                                19

3.1   Updating variables . . . . . . . . . . . . . . . . . . . . . . . .   19

3.2   Kinds of error . . . . . . . . . . . . . . . . . . . . . . . . . . .   20

3.3   Absolute and relative error  . . . . . . . . . . . . . . . . . . .   20

3.4   for loops . . . . . . . . . . . . . . . . . . . . . . . . . . . . . .   21

3.5   plotting  . . . . . . . . . . . . . . . . . . . . . . . . . . . . . .   22

3.6   Sequences  . . . . . . . . . . . . . . . . . . . . . . . . . . . . .   23

3.7   Series  . . . . . . . . . . . . . . . . . . . . . . . . . . . . . . .   23

3.8   Generalization  . . . . . . . . . . . . . . . . . . . . . . . . . .   24

3.9   Glossary . . . . . . . . . . . . . . . . . . . . . . . . . . . . . .   25

3.10  Exercises  . . . . . . . . . . . . . . . . . . . . . . . . . . . . .   26

## 4   Vectors                                                               27

4.1   Checking preconditions . . . . . . . . . . . . . . . . . . . . . .   27

4.2   if . . . . . . . . . . . . . . . . . . . . . . . . . . . . . . . . . .   28

4.3   Relational operators  . . . . . . . . . . . . . . . . . . . . . . .   28

4.4   Logical operators . . . . . . . . . . . . . . . . . . . . . . . . .   29

4.5   Vectors  . . . . . . . . . . . . . . . . . . . . . . . . . . . . . .   30

4.6   Vector arithmetic . . . . . . . . . . . . . . . . . . . . . . . . .   30

4.7   Everything is a matrix . . . . . . . . . . . . . . . . . . . . . . .   31

4.8   Indices . . . . . . . . . . . . . . . . . . . . . . . . . . . . . . .   33

4.9   Indexing errors  . . . . . . . . . . . . . . . . . . . . . . . . . .   33

4.10  Vectors and sequences . . . . . . . . . . . . . . . . . . . . . . .   34

4.11  Plotting vectors . . . . . . . . . . . . . . . . . . . . . . . . . .   35

4.12  Reduce . . . . . . . . . . . . . . . . . . . . . . . . . . . . . . .   35

4.13  Apply . . . . . . . . . . . . . . . . . . . . . . . . . . . . . . . .   36

4.14  Search . . . . . . . . . . . . . . . . . . . . . . . . . . . . . . .   36

4.15  Spoiling the fun . . . . . . . . . . . . . . . . . . . . . . . . . .   38

4.16  Glossary . . . . . . . . . . . . . . . . . . . . . . . . . . . . . .   38

4.17  Exercises  . . . . . . . . . . . . . . . . . . . . . . . . . . . . .   39

**5  Functions**                                                        **41**

   5.1  Name Collisions . . . . . . . . . . . . . . . . . . . . . . . . . 41

   5.2  Functions . . . . . . . . . . . . . . . . . . . . . . . . . . . . 41

   5.3  Documentation . . . . . . . . . . . . . . . . . . . . . . . . . 43

   5.4  Function names . . . . . . . . . . . . . . . . . . . . . . . . . 44

   5.5  Multiple input variables . . . . . . . . . . . . . . . . . . . . 45

   5.6  Logical functions . . . . . . . . . . . . . . . . . . . . . . . . 46

   5.7  An incremental development example . . . . . . . . . . . . . 47

   5.8  Nested loops . . . . . . . . . . . . . . . . . . . . . . . . . . 47

   5.9  Conditions and flags . . . . . . . . . . . . . . . . . . . . . . 49

   5.10 Encapsulation and generalization . . . . . . . . . . . . . . . 50

   5.11 A misstep . . . . . . . . . . . . . . . . . . . . . . . . . . . . 51

   5.12 `continue` . . . . . . . . . . . . . . . . . . . . . . . . . . . . 52

   5.13 Mechanism and leap of faith . . . . . . . . . . . . . . . . . . 53

   5.14 Glossary . . . . . . . . . . . . . . . . . . . . . . . . . . . . . 54

   5.15 Exercises . . . . . . . . . . . . . . . . . . . . . . . . . . . . . 54

**6  Zero-finding**                                                     **55**

   6.1  Why functions? . . . . . . . . . . . . . . . . . . . . . . . . . 55

   6.2  Maps . . . . . . . . . . . . . . . . . . . . . . . . . . . . . . . 55

   6.3  A note on notation . . . . . . . . . . . . . . . . . . . . . . . 56

   6.4  Nonlinear equations . . . . . . . . . . . . . . . . . . . . . . 56

   6.5  Zero-finding . . . . . . . . . . . . . . . . . . . . . . . . . . . 58

   6.6  `fzero` . . . . . . . . . . . . . . . . . . . . . . . . . . . . . . 59

   6.7  What could go wrong? . . . . . . . . . . . . . . . . . . . . . 60

   6.8  Finding an initial guess . . . . . . . . . . . . . . . . . . . . . 62

   6.9  More name collisions . . . . . . . . . . . . . . . . . . . . . . 62

   6.10 Debugging in four acts . . . . . . . . . . . . . . . . . . . . . 63

   6.11 Glossary . . . . . . . . . . . . . . . . . . . . . . . . . . . . . 64

   6.12 Exercises . . . . . . . . . . . . . . . . . . . . . . . . . . . . . 65

**7  Functions of vectors**                                                          **67**

   7.1  Functions and files . . . . . . . . . . . . . . . . . . . . . . . . . . 67

   7.2  Physical modeling . . . . . . . . . . . . . . . . . . . . . . . . . . 68

   7.3  Vectors as input variables . . . . . . . . . . . . . . . . . . . . . . 69

   7.4  Vectors as output variables . . . . . . . . . . . . . . . . . . . . . 70

   7.5  Vectorizing your functions . . . . . . . . . . . . . . . . . . . . . 70

   7.6  Sums and differences . . . . . . . . . . . . . . . . . . . . . . . . . 71

   7.7  Products and ratios . . . . . . . . . . . . . . . . . . . . . . . . . . 72

   7.8  Existential quantification . . . . . . . . . . . . . . . . . . . . . . 73

   7.9  Universal quantification . . . . . . . . . . . . . . . . . . . . . . . 74

   7.10 Logical vectors . . . . . . . . . . . . . . . . . . . . . . . . . . . . 74

   7.11 Glossary . . . . . . . . . . . . . . . . . . . . . . . . . . . . . . . . 75

**8  Ordinary Differential Equations**                                               **77**

   8.1  Differential equations . . . . . . . . . . . . . . . . . . . . . . . . 77

   8.2  Euler's method . . . . . . . . . . . . . . . . . . . . . . . . . . . . 78

   8.3  Another note on notation . . . . . . . . . . . . . . . . . . . . . . 79

   8.4  `ode45` . . . . . . . . . . . . . . . . . . . . . . . . . . . . . . . . 80

   8.5  Multiple output variables . . . . . . . . . . . . . . . . . . . . . . 82

   8.6  Analytic or numerical? . . . . . . . . . . . . . . . . . . . . . . . . 83

   8.7  What can go wrong? . . . . . . . . . . . . . . . . . . . . . . . . . 84

   8.8  Stiffness . . . . . . . . . . . . . . . . . . . . . . . . . . . . . . . . 85

   8.9  Glossary . . . . . . . . . . . . . . . . . . . . . . . . . . . . . . . . 86

   8.10 Exercises . . . . . . . . . . . . . . . . . . . . . . . . . . . . . . . . 87

**9  Systems of ODEs**                                                               **89**

   9.1  Matrices . . . . . . . . . . . . . . . . . . . . . . . . . . . . . . . . 89

   9.2  Row and column vectors . . . . . . . . . . . . . . . . . . . . . . . 90

   9.3  The transpose operator . . . . . . . . . . . . . . . . . . . . . . . 91

   9.4  Lotka-Voltera . . . . . . . . . . . . . . . . . . . . . . . . . . . . . 91

   9.5  What can go wrong? . . . . . . . . . . . . . . . . . . . . . . . . . 94

   9.6  Output matrices . . . . . . . . . . . . . . . . . . . . . . . . . . . . 94

   9.7  Glossary . . . . . . . . . . . . . . . . . . . . . . . . . . . . . . . . 95

   9.8  Exercises . . . . . . . . . . . . . . . . . . . . . . . . . . . . . . . . 96

**10 Second-order systems** ........................................................ **97**

10.1 Nested functions . . . . . . . . . . . . . . . . . . . . . . . . . . . . . . . . 97

10.2 Newtonian motion . . . . . . . . . . . . . . . . . . . . . . . . . . . . . . 98

10.3 Freefall . . . . . . . . . . . . . . . . . . . . . . . . . . . . . . . . . . . . 99

10.4 Air resistance . . . . . . . . . . . . . . . . . . . . . . . . . . . . . . . . 100

10.5 Parachute! . . . . . . . . . . . . . . . . . . . . . . . . . . . . . . . . . . 101

10.6 Two dimensions . . . . . . . . . . . . . . . . . . . . . . . . . . . . . . . 102

10.7 What could go wrong? . . . . . . . . . . . . . . . . . . . . . . . . . . . 103

10.8 Glossary . . . . . . . . . . . . . . . . . . . . . . . . . . . . . . . . . . . 105

10.9 Exercises . . . . . . . . . . . . . . . . . . . . . . . . . . . . . . . . . . . 105

**11 Optimization and Interpolation** ........................................... **107**

11.1 ODE Events . . . . . . . . . . . . . . . . . . . . . . . . . . . . . . . . . 107

11.2 Optimization . . . . . . . . . . . . . . . . . . . . . . . . . . . . . . . . 108

11.3 Golden section search . . . . . . . . . . . . . . . . . . . . . . . . . . . 108

11.4 Discrete and continuous maps . . . . . . . . . . . . . . . . . . . . . . 111

11.5 Interpolation . . . . . . . . . . . . . . . . . . . . . . . . . . . . . . . . 112

11.6 Interpolating the inverse function . . . . . . . . . . . . . . . . . . . . 113

11.7 Field mice . . . . . . . . . . . . . . . . . . . . . . . . . . . . . . . . . . 115

11.8 Glossary . . . . . . . . . . . . . . . . . . . . . . . . . . . . . . . . . . . 116

11.9 Exercises . . . . . . . . . . . . . . . . . . . . . . . . . . . . . . . . . . . 116

**12 Vectors as vectors** ............................................................ **117**

12.1 What's a vector? . . . . . . . . . . . . . . . . . . . . . . . . . . . . . . 117

12.2 Dot and cross products . . . . . . . . . . . . . . . . . . . . . . . . . . 119

12.3 Celestial mechanics . . . . . . . . . . . . . . . . . . . . . . . . . . . . . 119

12.4 Animation . . . . . . . . . . . . . . . . . . . . . . . . . . . . . . . . . . 120

12.5 Conservation of Energy . . . . . . . . . . . . . . . . . . . . . . . . . . 122

12.6 What is a model for? . . . . . . . . . . . . . . . . . . . . . . . . . . . . 123

12.7 Glossary . . . . . . . . . . . . . . . . . . . . . . . . . . . . . . . . . . . 123

12.8 Exercises . . . . . . . . . . . . . . . . . . . . . . . . . . . . . . . . . . . 124

# Chapter 1

# Variables and values

## 1.1 A glorified calculator

At heart, MATLAB is a glorified calculator. When you start MATLAB you will see a window entitled MATLAB that contains smaller windows entitled Current Directory, Command History and Command Window. The Command Window runs the MATLAB **interpreter**, which allows you to type MATLAB **commands**, then executes them and prints the result.

Initially, the Command Window contains a welcome message with information about the version of MATLAB you are running, followed by a chevron:

```
>>
```

which is the MATLAB **prompt**; that is, this symbol prompts you to enter a command.

The simplest kind of command is a mathematical **expression**, which is made up of **operands** (like numbers, for example) and **operators** (like the plus sign, +).

If you type an expression and then press Enter (or Return), MATLAB **evaluates** the expression and prints the result.

```
>> 2 + 1
ans = 3
```

Just to be clear, in the example above, MATLAB printed >>; I typed 2 + 1 and then hit Enter, and MATLAB printed ans = 3. And when I say "printed," I really mean "displayed on the screen," which might be confusing, but it's the way people talk.

An expression can contain any number of operators and operands. You don't have to put spaces between them; some people do and some people don't.

```
>> 1+2+3+4+5+6+7+8+9
ans = 45
```

Speaking of spaces, you might have noticed that MATLAB puts some space between ans = and the result. In my examples I will leave it out to save paper.

The other arithmetic operators are pretty much what you would expect. Subtraction is denoted by a minus sign, -; multiplication by an asterisk, * (sometimes pronounced "splat"); division by a forward slash /.

```
>> 2*3 - 4/5
ans = 5.2000
```

The order of operations is what you would expect from basic algebra: multiplication and division happen before addition and subtraction. If you want to override the order of operations, you can use parentheses.

```
>> 2 * (3-4) / 5
ans = -0.4000
```

When I added the parentheses I also changed the spacing to make the grouping of operands clearer to a human reader. This is the first of many style guidelines I will recommend for making your programs easier to read. Style doesn't change what the program does; the MATLAB interpreter doesn't check for style. But human readers do, and the most important human who will read your code is you.

And that brings us to the First Theorem of debugging:

Readable code is debuggable code.

It is worth spending some time to make your code pretty, if it saves you time debugging!

The other common operator is exponentiation, which uses the ^ symbol, sometimes pronounced "carat" or "hat". So 2 raised to the 16th power is

```
>> 2^16
ans = 65536
```

As in basic algebra, exponentiation happens before multiplication and division, but again, you can use parentheses to override the order of operations.

## 1.2   Math functions

MATLAB knows how to compute pretty much every math function you've heard of. It knows all the trigonometric functions; here's how you use them:

```
>> sin(1)
ans = 0.8415
```

This command is an example of a **function call**. The name of the function is `sin`, which is the usual abbreviation for the trigonometric sine. The value in parentheses is called the **argument**. All the trig functions in MATLAB work in radians.

Some functions take more than one argument, in which case they are separated by commas. For example, `atan2` computes the inverse tangent, which is the angle in radians between the positive x-axis and the point with the given $y$ and $x$ coordinates.

```
>> atan2(1,1)
ans = 0.7854
```

If that bit of trigonometry isn't familiar to you, don't worry about it. It's just an example of a function with multiple arguments.

MATLAB also provides exponential functions, like `exp`, which computes $e$ raised to the given power. So `exp(1)` is just $e$.

```
>> exp(1)
ans = 2.7183
```

The inverse of `exp` is `log`, which computes the logarithm base $e$:

```
>> log(exp(3))
ans = 3
```

This example also demonstrates that function calls can be **nested**; that is, you can use the result from one function as an argument for another.

More generally, you can use a function call as an operand in an expression.

```
>> sqrt(sin(0.5)^2 + cos(0.5)^2)
ans = 1
```

As you probably guessed, `sqrt` computes the square root.

There are lots of other math functions, but this is not meant to be a reference manual. To learn about other functions, you should read the documentation.

## 1.3   Documentation

MATLAB comes with two forms of online documentation, `help` and `doc`.

The help command works from the Command Window; just type `help` followed by the name of a command.

```
>> help sin
 SIN    Sine of argument in radians.
    SIN(X) is the sine of the elements of X.

    See also asin, sind.

    Overloaded functions or methods (ones with the same name in other
        directories) help sym/sin.m

    Reference page in Help browser
        doc sin
```

Unfortunately, this documentation is not beginner-friendly.

One gotcha is that the name of the function appears in the help page in capital letters, but if you type it like that in MATLAB, you get an error:

```
>> SIN(1)
??? Undefined command/function 'SIN'.
```

Another problem is that the help page uses vocabulary you don't know yet. For example, "the elements of X" won't make sense until we get to vectors and matrices a few chapters from now.

The doc pages are usually better. If you type `doc sin`, a browser appears with more detailed information about the function, including examples of how to use it. The examples often use vectors and arrays, so they may not make sense yet, but you can get a preview of what's coming.

## 1.4   Variables

One of the features that makes MATLAB more powerful than a calculator is the ability to give a name to a value. A named value is called a **variable**.

MATLAB comes with a few predefined variables. For example[1], the name `pi` refers to the mathematical quantity $\pi$, which is approximately

```
>> pi
ans = 3.1416
```

And if you do anything with complex numbers, you might find it convenient that both `i` and `j` are predefined as the square root of $-1$.

You can use a variable name anywhere you can use a number, as an operand in an expression:

```
>> pi * 3^2
ans = 28.2743
```

or as an argument to a function:

```
>> sin(pi/2)
ans = 1

>> exp(i * pi)
ans = -1.0000 + 0.0000i
```

As the second example shows, many MATLAB functions work with complex numbers. This example demonstrates Euler's Equality: $e^{i\pi} = -1$.

Whenever you evaluate an expression, MATLAB assigns the result to a variable named **ans**. You can use **ans** in a subsequent calculation as shorthand for "the value of the previous expression".

```
>> 3^2 + 4^2
ans = 25

>> sqrt(ans)
ans = 5
```

But keep in mind that the value of **ans** changes every time you evaluate an expression.

---

[1]Technically `pi` is a function, not a variable, but for now it's best to pretend.

## 1.5   Assignment statements

You can create your own variables, and give them values, with an **assignment statement**. The assignment operator is the equals sign, =.

```
>> x = 6 * 7
x = 42
```

This example creates a new variable named x and assigns it the value of the expression 6 * 7. MATLAB responds with the variable name and the computed value.

In every assignment statement, the left side has to be a legal variable name. The right side can be any expression, including function calls.

Almost any sequence of lower and upper case letters is a legal variable name. Some punctuation is also legal, but the underscore, _, is the only commonly used non-letter. Numbers are fine, but not at the beginning. Spaces are not allowed. Variable names are "case sensitive", so x and X are different variables.

```
>> fibonacci0 = 1;

>> LENGTH = 10;

>> first_name = 'allen'
first_name = allen
```

The first two examples demonstrate the use of the semi-colon, which suppresses the output from a command. In this case MATLAB creates the variables and assigns them values, but displays nothing.

The third example demonstrates that not everything in MATLAB is a number. A sequence of characters in single quotes is a **string**.

Although i, j and pi are predefined, you are free to reassign them. It is common to use i and j for other purposes, but it is probably not a good idea to change the value of pi!

## 1.6   Why variables?

The most common reasons to use variables are

- To avoid recomputing a value that is used repeatedly. For example, if you are performing computations involving $e$, you might want to compute it once and save the result.

```
>> e = exp(1)
e = 2.7183
```

- To make the connection between the code and the underlying mathematics more apparent. If you are computing the area of a circle, you might want to use a variable named r:

```
>> r = 3
r = 3

>> area = pi * r^2
area = 28.2743
```

That way your code resembles the familiar formula $\pi r^2$.

- To break a long computation into a sequence of steps. Suppose you are evaluating a big, hairy expression like this:

```
ans = ((x - theta) * sqrt(2 * pi) * sigma) ^ -1 * ...
exp(-1/2 * (log(x - theta) - zeta)^2 / sigma^2)
```

You can use an ellipsis to break the expression into multiple lines. Just type ... at the end of the first line and continue on the next.

But often it is better to break the computation into a sequence of steps and assign intermediate results to variables.

```
shiftx = x - theta
denom = shiftx * sqrt(2 * pi) * sigma
temp = (log(shiftx) - zeta) / sigma
exponent = -1/2 * temp^2
ans = exp(exponent) / denom
```

The names of the intermediate variables explain their role in the computation. shiftx is the value of x shifted by theta. It should be no surprise that exponent is the argument of exp, and denom ends up in the denominator. Choosing informative names makes the code easier to read and understand (see the First Theorem of Debugging).


## 1.7   Errors

It's early, but now would be a good time to start making errors. Whenever you learn a new feature, you should try to make as many errors as possible, as soon as possible.

When you make deliberate errors, you get to see what the error messages look like. Later, when you make accidental errors, you will know what the messages mean.

A common error for beginning programmers is leaving out the * for multiplication.

```
>> area = pi r^2
??? area = pi r^2
          |
Error: Unexpected MATLAB expression.
```

The error message indicates that, after seeing the operand pi, MATLAB was "expecting" to see an operator, like *. Instead, it got a variable name, which is the "unexpected expression" indicated by the vertical line, | (which is called a "pipe").

Another common error is to leave out the parentheses around the arguments of a function. For example, in math notation, it is common to write something like $\sin \pi$, but not in MATLAB.

```
>> sin pi
??? Function 'sin' is not defined for values of class 'char'.
```

The problem is that when you leave out the parentheses, MATLAB treats the argument as a string (rather than as an expression). In this case the `sin` function generates a reasonable error message, but in other cases the results can be baffling. For example, what do you think is going on here?

```
>> abs pi
ans =  112    105
```

There is a reason for this "feature", but rather than get into that now, let me suggest that you should *always* put parentheses around arguments.

This example also demonstrates the Second Theorem of Debugging:

> The only thing worse than getting an error message is *not* getting an error message.

Beginning programmers hate error messages and do everything they can to make them go away. Experienced programmers know that error messages are your friend. They can be hard to understand, and even misleading, but it is worth making some effort to understand them.

Here's another common rookie error. If you were translating the following mathematical expression into MATLAB:

$$\frac{1}{2\sqrt{\pi}}$$

You might be tempted to write something like this:

```
1 / 2 * sqrt(pi)
```

But that would be wrong. So very wrong.

## 1.8    Floating-point arithmetic

In mathematics, there are several kinds of numbers: integer, real, rational, irrational, imaginary, complex, etc. MATLAB only has one kind of number, called (for reasons I won't explain here) **floating-point**.

You might have noticed that MATLAB expresses values in decimal notation. So, for example, the rational number $1/3$ is represented by the floating-point value

```
>> 1/3
ans = 0.3333
```

which is only approximately correct. It's not quite as bad as it seems; MATLAB uses more digits than it shows by default. You can change the `format` to see the other digits.

```
>> format long
>> 1/3
ans = 0.33333333333333
```

Internally, MATLAB uses the IEEE double-precision floating-point format, which provides about 15 significant digits of precision (in base 10). Leading and trailing zeros don't count as "significant" digits, so MATLAB can represent large and small numbers with the same precision.

Very large and very small values are displayed in scientific notation.

```
>> factorial(100)
ans = 9.332621544394410e+157
```

The e in this notation is *not* the transcendental number known as $e$; it is just an abbreviation for "exponent". So this means that 100! is approximately $9.33 \times 10^{157}$. The exact solution is a 158-digit integer, but we only know the first 16 digits.

You can enter numbers using the same notation.

```
>> speed_of_light = 3.0e8
speed_of_light = 300000000
```

Although MATLAB can handle large numbers, there is a limit. The predefined variables realmax and realmin contain the largest and smallest numbers that MATLAB can handle[2].

```
>> realmax
ans = 1.797693134862316e+308
```

```
>> realmin
ans = 2.225073858507201e-308
```

If the result of a computation is too big, MATLAB "rounds up" to infinity.

```
>> factorial(170)
ans = 7.257415615307994e+306
```

```
>> factorial(171)
ans = Inf
```

Division by zero also returns Inf, but in this case MATLAB gives you a warning because in many circles division by zero is considered undefined.

```
>> 1/0
Warning: Divide by zero.

ans = Inf
```

A warning is like an error message without teeth; the computation is allowed to continue. Allowing Inf to propagate through a computation doesn't always do what you expect, but if you are careful with how you use it, Inf can be quite useful.

For operations that are truly undefined, MATLAB returns NaN, which stands for "not a number".

---

[2]The names of these variables are misleading; floating-point numbers are sometimes, wrongly, called "real".

```
>> 0/0
Warning: Divide by zero.

ans = NaN
```

## 1.9  Comments

Along with the commands that make up a program, it is useful to include comments that
provide additional information about the program in natural language. The percent symbol
% separates the comments from the code.

```
>> speed_of_light = 3.0e8      % meters per second
speed_of_light = 300000000
```

The comment runs from the percent symbol to the end of the line. In this case it specifies
the units of the value. In an ideal world, MATLAB would keep track of units and propagate
them through the computation, but for now that burden falls on the programmer.

Comments have no effect on the execution of the program. They are there for human
readers. Good comments make programs more readable, but bad comments are useless or
(even worse) misleading.

Avoid comments that are redundant with the code:

```
>> x = 5          % assign the value 5 to x
```

Good comments provide additional information that is not in the code, like units in the
example above, or the meaning of a variable:

```
>> p = 0          % position from the origin in meters
>> v = 100        % velocity in meters / second
>> a = -9.8       % acceleration of gravity in meters / second^2
```

If you use longer variable names, you might not need explanatory comments, but there is
a tradeoff: longer code can become harder to read. Also, if you are translating from math
that uses short variable names, it can be useful to make your program consistent with your
math.

## 1.10  Glossary

**interpreter:** The program that reads and executes MATLAB code.

**command:** A line of MATLAB code executed by the interpreter.

**prompt:** The symbol the interpreter prints to indicate that it is waiting for you to type a
command.

**operator:** One of the symbols, like * and +, that represent mathematical operations.

**operand:** A number or variable that appears in an expression along with operators.

**expression:** A sequence of operands and operators that specifies a mathematical computation and yields a value.

**value:** The numerical result of a computation.

**evaluate:** To compute the value of an expression.

**order of operations:** The rules that specify which operations in an expression are per-
   formed first.

**function:** A named computation; for example log10 is the name of a function that computes logarithms in base 10.

**call:** To cause a function to execute and compute a result.

**function call:** A kind of command that executes a function.

**argument:** An expression that appears in a function call to specify the value the function
   operates on.

**nested function call:** An expression that uses the result from one function call as an
   argument for another.

**variable:** A named value.

**assignment statement:** A command that creates a new variable (if necessary) and gives
   it a value.

**string:** A value that consists of a sequence of characters (as opposed to a number).

**floating-point:** The kind of number MATLAB works with. All floating-point numbers can
   be represented with about 16 significant decimal digits (unlike mathematical integers
   and reals).

**scientific notation:** A format for typing and displaying large and small numbers; e.g.
   3.0e8, which represents $3.0 \times 10^8$ or 300,000,000.

**comment:** Part of a program that provides additional information about the program, but
   does not affect its execution.

## 1.11   Exercises

**Exercise 1.1**   *Write a MATLAB expression that evaluates the following math expression.
You can assume that the variables* mu, sigma *and* x *already exist.*

$$\frac{e^{-\left(\frac{x-\mu}{\sigma\sqrt{2}}\right)^2}}{\sigma\sqrt{2\pi}} \tag{1.1}$$

*Note: you can't use Greek letters in MATLAB; when translating math expressions with
Greek letters, it is common to write out the name of the letter (assuming you know it).*

# Chapter 2

# Scripts

## 2.1 M-files

So far we have typed all of our programs "at the prompt," which is fine if you are not writing more than a few lines. Beyond that, you will want to store your program in a **script** and then execute the script.

A script is a file that contains MATLAB code. These files are also called "M-files" because they use the extension `.m`, which is short for MATLAB.

You can create and edit scripts with any text editor or word processor, but the simplest way is by selecting New→M-File from the File menu. A window appears running a text editor specially designed for MATLAB.

Type the following code in the editor

```
x = 5
```

and then press the (outdated) floppy disk icon, or select Save from the File menu. Either way, a dialog box appears where you can choose the file name and the directory where it should go. Change the name to `myscript.m` and leave the directory unchanged.

By default, MATLAB will store your script in a directory that is on the **search path**, which is the list of directories MATLAB searches for scripts.

Go back to the Command Window and type `myscript` (without the extension) at the prompt. MATLAB executes your script and displays the result.

```
>> myscript
x = 5
```

When you run a script, MATLAB executes the commands in the M-File, one after another, exactly as if you had typed them at the prompt.

If something goes wrong and MATLAB can't find your script, you will get an error message like:

```
>> myscript
??? Undefined function or variable 'myscript'.
```

In this case you can either save your script again in a directory that is on the search path, or modify the search path to include the directory where you keep your scripts. You'll have to consult the documentation for the details (sorry!).

Keeping track of your scripts can be a pain. To keep things simple, for now, I suggest keeping all of your scripts in the default directory.

**Exercise 2.1** *The Fibonacci sequence, denoted $F$, is described by the equations $F_1 = 1$, $F_2 = 1$, and for $i \geq 3$, $F_i = F_{i-1} + F_{i-2}$. The terms of this sequence occur naturally in many plants, particularly those with petals or scales arranged in the form of a logarithmic spiral.*

*The following expression computes the nth Fibonacci number:*

$$F_n \approx \frac{1}{\sqrt{5}} \left[ \left( \frac{1 + \sqrt{5}}{2} \right)^n - \left( \frac{1 - \sqrt{5}}{2} \right)^n \right] \tag{2.1}$$

*Translate this expression into MATLAB and store your code in a file named* `fibonacci1`. *At the prompt, set the value of* `n` *to 10 and then run your script. The last line of your script should assign the value of $F_n$ to* `ans`. *(The correct value of $F_{10}$ is 55).*

## 2.2   Why scripts?

The most common reasons to use scripts are

- When you are writing more than a couple of lines of code, it might take a few tries to get everything right. Putting your code in a script makes it easier to edit than typing it at the prompt.

  On the other hand, it can be a pain to switch back and forth between the Command Window and the Editor. Try to arrange your windows so you can see the Editor and the Command Window at the same time, and use the Tab key or the mouse to switch between them.

- If you choose good names for your scripts, you will be able to remember which script does what, and you might be able to reuse a script from one project to the next.

- If you run a script repeatedly, it is faster to type the name of the script than to retype the code!

Unfortunately, the great power of scripts comes with great responsibility, which is that you have to make sure that the code you are running is the code you think you are running.

First, whenever you edit your script, you have to save it before you run it. If you forget to save it, you will be running the old version.

Also, whenever you start an new script, start with something simple, like x=5 that produces a visible effect. Then run your script and confirm that you get what you expect. MATLAB comes with a lot of predefined functions. It is easy to write a script that has the same name as a MATLAB function, and if you are not careful, you might find yourself running the MATLAB function instead of your script.

Either way, if the code you are running is not the code you are looking at, you will find debugging a frustrating exercise! And that brings us to the Third Theorem of Debugging

> You must always be 100% sure that the code you are running is the code you think you are running.

## 2.3   The workspace

The variables you create are stored in the **workspace**, which is a set of variables and their values. The who command prints the names of the variables in the workspace.

```
>> x=5;
>> y=7;
>> z=9;
>> who

Your variables are:

x  y  z
```

The clear command removes variables.

```
>> clear y
>> who

Your variables are:

x  z
```

To display the value of a variable, you can use the disp function.

```
>> disp(z)
     9
```

But it's easier to just type the variable name.

```
>> z
z = 9
```

(Strictly speaking, the name of a variable is an expression, so evaluating it should assign a value to ans, but MATLAB seems to handle this as a special case.)

## 2.4   More errors

Again, when you try something new, you should make a few mistakes on purpose so you'll recognize them later.

The most common error with scripts is to run a script without creating the necessary variables. For example, `fibonacci1` requires you to assign a value to **n**. If you don't:

```
>> fibonacci1
??? Undefined function or variable "n".

Error in ==> fibonacci1 at 4
diff = t1^(n+1) - t2^(n+1);
```

The details of this message might be different for you, depending on what's in your script. But the general idea is that n is undefined. Notice that MATLAB tells you what line of your program the error is in, and displays the line.

This information can be helpful, but beware! MATLAB is telling you where the error was discovered, not where the error is. In this case, the error is not in the script at all; it is, in a sense, in the workspace.

Which brings us to the Fourth Theorem of Debugging:

> Error messages tell you where the problem was discovered, not where it was caused.

The object of the game is to find the cause and fix it—not just to make the error message go away.

## 2.5   Pre- and post-conditions

Every script should contain a comment that explains what it does, and what the requirements are for the workspace. For example, I might put something like this at the beginning of `fibonacci1`:

```
% Computes the nth Fibonacci number.
% Precondition: you must assign a value to n before running
% this script.  Postcondition: the result is stored in ans.
```

A **precondition** is something that must be true, when the script starts, in order for it to work correctly. A **postcondition** is something that will be true when the script completes.

If there is a comment at the beginning of a script, MATLAB assumes it is the documentation for the script, so if you type `help fibonacci1`, you get the contents of the comment (without the percent signs).

```
>> help fibonacci1
  Computes the nth Fibonacci number.
  Precondition: you must assign a value to n before running
  this script.  Postcondition: the result is stored in ans.
```

That way, scripts that you write behave just like predefined scripts. You can even use the `doc` command to see your comment in the Help Window.

## 2.6    Assignment and equality

In mathematics the equals sign means that the two sides of the equation have the same value. In MATLAB an assignment statement *looks* like a mathematical equality, but it's not.

One difference is that the sides of an assignment statement are not interchangeable. The right side can be any legal expression, but the left side has to be a variable, which is called the **target** of the assignment. So this is legal:

```
>> y = 1;
>> x = y+1
x = 2
```

But this is not:

```
>> y+1 = x
??? y+1 = x
          |
Error: The expression to the left of the equals sign is not a valid
target for an assignment.
```

In this case the error message is pretty helpful, as long as you know what a "target" is.

Another difference is that an assignment statement is only temporary, in the following sense. When you assign x = y+1, you get the *current* value of y. If y changes later, x does not get updated.

A third difference is that a mathematical equality is a statement that may or may not be true. For example, $y = y + 1$ is a statement that happens to be false for all real values of $y$. In MATLAB, y = y+1 is a sensible and useful assignment statement. It reads the current value of y, adds one, and replaces the old value with the new value.

```
>> y = 1;
>> y = y+1
y = 2
```

When you read MATLAB code, you might find it helpful to pronounce the equals sign "gets" rather than "equals." So x = y+1 is pronounced "x gets the value of y plus one."

To test your understanding of assignment statements, try this exercise:

**Exercise 2.2**   *Write a few lines of code that swap the values of x and y. Put your code in a script called* swap *and test it.*

## 2.7    Incremental development

When you start writing scripts that are more than a few lines, you might find yourself spending more and more time debugging. The more code you write before you start debugging, the harder it is to find the problem.

**Incremental development** is a way of programming that tries to minimize the pain of debugging. The fundamental steps are

1. Always start with a working program. If you have an example from a book or a program you wrote that is similar to what you are working on, start with that. Otherwise, start with something you *know* is correct, like x=5. Run the program and confirm that you are running the program you think you are running.

   This step is important, because in most environments there are lots of little things that can trip you up when you start a new project. Get them out of the way so you can focus on programming.

2. Make one small, testable change at a time. A "testable" change is one that displays something on the screen (or has some other effect) that you can check. Ideally, you should know what the correct answer is, or be able to check it by performing another computation.

3. Run the program and see if the change worked. If so, go back to Step 2. If not, you will have to do some debugging, but if the change you made was small, it shouldn't take long to find the problem.

When this process works, you will find that your changes usually work the first time, or the problem is obvious. That's a good thing, and it brings us to the Fifth Theorem of Debugging:

> The best kind of debugging is the kind you don't have to do.

In practice, there are two problems with incremental development:

- Sometimes you have to write some extra code in order to generate visible output that you can check. This extra code is called **scaffolding** because you use it to build the program and then remove it when you are done. But time you save on debugging is almost always worth the time you spend on scaffolding.

- When you are getting started, it is usually not obvious how to choose the steps that get from x=5 to the program you are trying to write. There is an extended example in Section 5.7.

If you find yourself writing more than a few lines of code before you start testing, and you are spending a lot of time debugging, you should try incremental development.

## 2.8   Unit testing

In large software projects, **unit testing** is the process of testing software components in isolation before putting them together.

The programs we have seen so far are not big enough to need unit testing, but the same principle applies when you are working with a new function or a new language feature for the first time. You should test it in isolation before you put it into your program.

For example, suppose you know that x is the sine of some angle and you want to find the angle. You find the MATLAB function asin, and you are pretty sure it computes the inverse sine function. Pretty sure is not good enough; you want to be very sure.

Since we know $\sin 0 = 0$, we could try

```
>> asin(0)
ans = 0
```

which is correct. Also, we know that the sine of 90 degrees is 1, so if we try `asin(1)`, we expect the answer to be 90, right?

```
>> asin(1)
ans = 1.5708
```

Oops. We forgot that the trig functions in MATLAB work in radians, not degrees. So the correct answer is $\pi/2$, which we can confirm by dividing through by `pi`:

```
>> asin(1) / pi
ans = 0.5000
```

With this kind of unit testing, you are not really checking for errors in MATLAB, you are checking your understanding. If you make an error because you are confused about how MATLAB works, it might take a long time to find, because when you look at the code, it looks right.

Which brings us to the Sixth Theorem of Debugging:

> The worst bugs aren't in your code; they are in your head.

## 2.9   Glossary

**M-file:** A file that contains a MATLAB program.

**script:** An M-file that contains a sequence of MATLAB commands.

**search path:** The list of directories where MATLAB looks for M-files.

**workspace:** A set of variables and their values.

**precondition:** Something that must be true when the script starts, in order for it to work correctly.

**postcondition:** Something that will be true when the script completes.

**target:** The variable on the left side of an assignment statement.

**incremental development:** A way of programming by making a series of small, testable changes.

**scaffolding:** Code you write to help you program or debug, but which is not part of the finished program.

**unit testing:** A process of testing software by testing each component in isolation.

## 2.10   Exercises

**Exercise 2.3**   *Imagine that you are the owner of a car rental company with two locations, Albany and Boston. Some of your customers do "one-way rentals," picking up a car in Albany and returning it in Boston, or the other way around. Over time, you have observed that each week 5% of the cars in Albany are dropped off in Boston, and 3% of the cars in Boston get dropped off in Albany. At the beginning of the year, there are 150 cars at each location.*

*Write a script called* car_update *that updates the number of cars in each location from one week to the next. The precondition is that the variables* a *and* b *contain the number of cars in each location at the beginning of the week. The postcondition is that* a *and* b *have been modified to reflect the number of cars that moved.*

*To test your program, initialize* a *and* b *at the prompt and then execute the script. The script should display the updated values of* a *and* b*, but not any intermediate variables.*

*Note: cars are countable things, so* a *and* b *should always be integer values. You might want to use the* round *function to compute the number of cars that move during each week.*

*If you execute your script repeatedly, you can simulate the passage of time from week to week. What do you think will happen to the number of cars? Will all the cars end up in one place? Will the number of cars reach an equilibrium, or will it oscillate from week to week?*

*In the next chapter we will see how to execute your script automatically, and how to plot the values of* a *and* b *versus time.*

# Chapter 3

# Loops

## 3.1 Updating variables

In Exercise 2.3, you might have been tempted to write something like

```
a = a - 0.05*a + 0.03*b
b = b + 0.05*a - 0.03*b
```

But that would be wrong, so very wrong. Why? The problem is that the first line changes the value of a, so when the second line runs, it gets the old value of b and the new value of a. As a result, the change in a is not always the same as the change in b, which violates the principle of Conversation of Cars!

One solution is to use temporary variables anew and bnew:

```
anew = a - 0.05*a + 0.03*b
bnew = b + 0.05*a - 0.03*b
a = anew
b = bnew
```

This has the effect of updating the variables "simultaneously;" that is, it reads both old values before writing either new value.

The following is an alternative solution that has the added advantage of simplifying the computation:

```
atob = 0.05*a - 0.03*b
a = a - atob
b = b + atob
```

It is easy to look at this code and confirm that it obeys Conversation of Cars. Even if the value of atob is wrong, at least the total number of cars is right. And that brings us to the Seventh Theorem of Debugging:

> The best way to avoid a bug is to make it impossible.

In this case, removing redundancy also eliminates the opportunity for a bug.

## 3.2  Kinds of error

There are four kinds of error:

**Syntax error:** You have written a MATLAB command that cannot execute because it
   violates one of the rules of syntax. For example, you can't have two operands in a
   row without an operator, so pi r^2 contains a syntax error. When MATLAB finds a
   syntax error, it prints an error message and stops running your program.

**Runtime error:** Your program starts running, but something goes wrong along the way.
   For example, if you try to access a variable that doesn't exist, that's a runtime error.
   When MATLAB detects the problem, it prints an error message and stops.

**Logical error:** Your program runs without generating any error messages, but it doesn't
   do the right thing. The problem in the previous section, where we changed the value
   of a before reading the old value, is a logical error.

**Numerical error:** Most computations in MATLAB are only approximately right. Most of
   the time the errors are small enough that we don't care, but in some cases the roundoff
   errors are a problem.

Syntax errors are usually the easiest. Sometimes the error messages are confusing, but
MATLAB can usually tell you where the error is, at least roughly.

Run time errors are harder because, as I mentioned before, MATLAB can tell you where it
detected the problem, but not what caused it.

Logical errors are hard because MATLAB can't help at all. Only you know what the program
is supposed to do, so only you can check it. From MATLAB's point of view, there's nothing
wrong with the program; the bug is in your head!

Numerical errors can be tricky because it's not clear whether the problem is your fault. For
most simple computations, MATLAB produces the floating-point value that is closest to
the exact solution, which means that the first 15 significant digits should be correct. But
some computations are ill-conditioned, which means that even if your program is correct,
the roundoff errors accumulate and the number of correct digits can be smaller. Sometimes
MATLAB can warn you that this is happening, but not always! Precision (the number of
digits in the answer) does not imply accuracy (the number of digits that are right).

## 3.3  Absolute and relative error

There are two ways of thinking about numerical errors, called **absolute** and **relative**.

An absolute error is just the difference between the correct value and the approximation.
We usually write the magnitude of the error, ignoring its sign, because it doesn't matter
whether the approximation is too high or too low.

For example, we might want to estimate 9! using the formula $\sqrt{18\pi}(9/e)^9$. The exact answer
is $9 \cdot 8 \cdot 7 \cdot 6 \cdot 5 \cdot 4 \cdot 3 \cdot 2 \cdot 1 = 362,880$. The approximation is $359,536.87$. The absolute error
is $3,343.13$.

At first glance, that sounds like a lot—we're off by three thousand—but it is worth taking into account the size of the thing we are estimating. For example, $3000 matters a lot if we are talking about my annual salary, but not at all if we are talking about the national debt.

A natural way to handle this problem is to use relative error, which is the error expressed as a fraction (or percentage) of the exact value. In this case, we would divide the error by 362,880, yielding .00921, which is just less than 1%. For many purposes, being off by 1% is good enough.

## 3.4   for loops

A **loop** is a part of a program that executes repeatedly; a **for loop** is the kind of loop that uses the `for` statement.

The simplest use of a `for` loop is to execute one or more lines a fixed number of times. For example, in the last chapter we wrote a script named `car_update` that simulates one week in the life of a rental car company. To simulate an entire year, we have to run it 52 times:

```
for i=1:52
    car_update
end
```

The first line looks like an assignment statement, and it is like an assignment statement, except that it runs more than once. The first time it runs, it creates the variable `i` and assigns it the value 1. The second time, `i` gets the value 2, and so on, up to 52.

The colon operator, `:`, specifies a **range** of integers. In the spirit of unit testing, you can create a range at the prompt:

```
>> 1:5
ans =   1     2     3     4     5
```

The variable you use in the for statement is called the **loop variable**. It is a common convention to use the names `i`, `j` and `k` as loop variables (except when you are using complex numbers, in which case you use i or j for $\sqrt{-1}$).

The statements inside the loop are called the **body**. By convention, they are indented to show that they are inside the loop, but the indentation does not actually affect the execution of the program. The end of the loop is officially marked by the **end** statement.

To see the loop in action you can run a loop that displays the loop variable:

```
>> for i=1:5
     i
end


i = 1
i = 2
i = 3
i = 4
i = 5
```

As this example shows, you *can* run a for loop from the command line, but it's much more common to put it in a script.

**Exercise 3.1** *Create a script named* car_loop *that uses a* for *loop to run* car_update *52 times. Remember that before you run* car_update, *you have to assign values to* a *and* b. *For this exercise, start with the values* a = 150 *and* b = 150.

*If everything goes smoothly, your script will display a long stream of numbers on the screen. But it is probably too long to fit, and even if it fit, it would be hard to interpret. A graph would be much better!*

## 3.5   plotting

plot is a versatile function for plotting points and lines on a two-dimensional graph. Unfortunately, it is so versatile that it can be hard to use (and hard to read the documentation!). We will start simple and work our way up.

To plot a single point, type

```
>> plot(1, 2)
```

A Figure Window should appear with a graph and a single, blue dot at $x$ position 1 and $y$ position 2. To make the dot more visible, you can specify a different shape:

```
>> plot(1, 2, 'o')
```

The letter in single quotes is a string that specifies how the point should be plotted. You can also specify the color:

```
>> plot(1, 2, 'ro')
```

r stands for red; the other colors include green, blue, cyan, magenta, yellow and black. Other shapes include +, *, x, s (for square), d (for diamond), and ^ (for a triangle).

When you use plot this way, it can only plot one point at a time. If you run plot again, it clears the figure before making the new plot. The hold command lets you override that behavior. hold on tells MATLAB not to clear the figure when it makes a new plot; hold off returns to the default behavior.

Try this:

```
>> hold on
>> plot(1, 1, 'o')
>> plot(2, 2, 'o')
```

You should see a figure with two points. MATLAB scales the plot automatically so that the axes run from the lowest value in the plot to the highest. So in this example the points are plotted in the corners.

**Exercise 3.2** *Modify* car_loop *so that each time through the loop it plots the value of* a *versus the value of* i.

*Once you get that working, modify it so it plots the values of* a *with red circles and the values of* b *with blue diamonds.*

*One more thing: if you use* `hold on` *to prevent MATLAB from clearing the figure, you might want to clear the figure yourself, from time to time, with the command* `clf`.

## 3.6   Sequences

In mathematics a **sequence** is a set of numbers that corresponds to the positive integers. The numbers in the sequence are called **elements**. In math notation, the elements are denoted with subscripts, so the first element of the series $A$ is $A_1$, followed by $A_2$, and so on.

`for` loops are a natural way to compute the elements of a sequence. As an example, in a geometric sequence, each element is a constant multiple of the previous element. As a more specific example, let's look at the sequence with $A_1 = 1$ and the ratio $A_{i+1} = A_i/2$, for all $i$. In other words, each element is half as big as the one before it.

The following loop computes the first 10 elements of $A$:

```
a = 1
for i=2:10
    a = a/2
end
```

Each time through the loop, we find the next value of `a` by dividing the previous value by 2. Notice that the loop range starts at 2 because the initial value of `a` corresponds to $A_1$, so the first time through the loop we are computing $A_2$.

Each time through the loop, we replace the previous element with the next, so at the end, `a` contains the 10th element. The other elements are displayed on the screen, but they are not saved in a variable. Later, we will see how to save all of the elements of a sequence in a vector.

This loop computes the sequence **recurrently**, which means that each element depends on the previous one. For this sequence it is also possible to compute the $i$th element **directly**, as a function of $i$, without using the previous element. In math notation, $A_i = A_1 r^{i-1}$.

**Exercise 3.3**   *Write a script named* `sequence` *that uses a loop to computes elements of $A$ directly.*

## 3.7   Series

In mathematics, a **series** is the sum of the elements of a sequence. It's a terrible name, because in common English, "sequence" and "series" mean pretty much the same thing, but in math, a sequence is a set of numbers, and a series is an expression (a sum) that has a single value. In math notation, a series is often written using the summation symbol $\sum$.

For example, the sum of the first 10 elements of $A$ is

$$\sum_{i=1}^{10} A_i$$

A `for` loop is a natural way to compute the value of this series:

```
A1 = 1;
total = 0;
for i=1:10
    a = A1 * 0.5^(i-1);
    total = total + a;
end
ans = total
```

A1 is the first element of the sequence, so each time through the loop a is the $i$th element.

The way we are using `total` is sometimes called an **accumulator**; that is, a variable that accumulates a result a little bit at a time. Before the loop we initialize it to 0. Each time through the loop we add in the $i$th element. At the end of the loop `total` contains the sum of the elements. Since that's the value we were looking for, we assign it to `ans`.

**Exercise 3.4**   *This example computes the terms of the series directly; as an exercise, write a script named* `series` *that computes the same sum by computing the elements recurrently. You will have to be careful about where you start and stop the loop.*

## 3.8   Generalization

As written, the previous example always adds up the first 10 elements of the sequence, but we might be curious to know what happens to `total` as we increase the number of terms in the sequence. If you have studied geometric series, you might know that this series converges on 2; that is, as the number of terms goes to infinity, the sum approaches 2 asymptotically.

To see if that's true for our program, we could replace the constant, 10, with a variable named **n**:

```
A1 = 1;
total = 0;
for i=1:n
    a = A1 * 0.5^(i-1);
    total = total + a;
end
ans = total
```

Now the script can compute any number of terms, with the precondition that you have to set n before you execute the script. Here's how you could run it with different values of **n**:

```
>> n=10; series
```

```
total = 1.99804687500000
```

```
>> n=20; series
```

```
total = 1.99999809265137
```

```
>> n=30; series
```

```
total = 1.99999999813735
```

```
>> n=40; series
```

```
total = 1.99999999999818
```
It sure looks like it's converging on 2.

Replacing a constant with a variable is called **generalization**. Instead of computing a fixed, specific number of terms, the new script is more general; it can compute any number of terms.

This is an important idea we will come back to when we talk about functions.

## 3.9   Glossary

**absolute error:** The difference between an approximation and an exact answer.

**relative error:** The difference between an approximation and an exact answer, expressed as a fraction or percentage of the exact answer.

**loop:** A part of a program that runs repeatedly.

**loop variable:** A variable, defined in a `for` statement, that gets assigned a different value each time through the loop.

**range:** The set of values assigned to the loop variable, often specified with the colon operator; for example `1:5`.

**body:** The statements inside the for loop that are run repeatedly.

**sequence:** In mathematics, a set of numbers that correspond to the positive integers.

**element:** A member of the set of numbers in a sequence.

**recurrently:** A way of computing the next element of a sequence based on previous elements.

**directly:** A way of computing an element in a sequence without using previous elements.

**series:** The sum of the elements in a sequence.

**accumulator:** A variable that is used to accumulate a result a little bit at a time.

**generalization:** A way to make a program more versatile, for example by replacing a specific value with a variable that can have any value.

## 3.10  Exercises

**Exercise 3.5**  *We have already seen the Fibonacci sequence, F, which is defined recurrently as*

$$F_i = F_{i-1} + F_{i-2}$$

*In order to get started, you have to specify the first two elements, but once you have those, you can compute the rest. The most common Fibonacci sequence starts with $F_1 = 1$ and $F_2 = 1$.*

*Write a script called* `fibonacci2` *that uses a for loop to compute the first 10 elements of this Fibonacci sequence. As a postcondition, your script should assign the 10th element to* `ans`.

*Now generalize your script so that it computes the nth element for any value of* `n`, *with the precondition that you have to set* `n` *before you run the script. To keep things simple for now, you can assume that* `n` *is greater than 2.*

*Hint: you will have to use two variables to keep track of the previous two elements of the sequence. You might want to call them* `prev1` *and* `prev2`. *Initially,* `prev1` = $F_1$ *and* `prev2` = $F_2$. *At the end of the loop, you will have to update* `prev1` *and* `prev2`; *think carefully about the order of the updates!*

**Exercise 3.6**  *Write a script named* `fib_plot` *that loops i through a range from 1 to 20, uses* `fibonacci2` *to compute Fibonacci numbers, and plots $F_i$ for each i with a series of red circles.*

# Chapter 4

# Vectors

## 4.1 Checking preconditions

Some of the loops in the previous chapter don't work if the value of **n** isn't set correctly before the loop runs. For example, this loop computes the sum of the first **n** elements of a geometric sequence:

```
A1 = 1;
total = 0;
for i=1:n
    a = A1 * 0.5^(i-1);
    total = total + a;
end
ans = total
```

It works for any positive value of **n**, but what if **n** is negative? In that case, you get:

```
total = 0
```

Why? Because the expression `1:-1` means "all the numbers from 1 to -1, counting up by 1." It's not immediately obvious what that should mean, but MATLAB's interpretation is that there aren't any numbers that fit that description, so the result is

```
>> 1:-1
```

```
ans = Empty matrix: 1-by-0
```

If the matrix is empty, you might expect it to be "0-by-0," but there you have it. In any case, if you loop over an empty range, the loop never runs at all, which is why in this example the value of `total` is zero for any negative value of **n**.

If you are sure that you will never make a mistake, and that the preconditions of your functions will always be satisfied, then you don't have to check. But for the rest of us, it is dangerous to write a script, like this one, that quietly produces the wrong answer (or at least a meaningless answer) if the input value is negative. A better alternative is to use an `if` statement.

## 4.2   if

The `if` statement allows you to check for certain conditions and execute statements if the conditions are met. In the previous example, we could write:

```
if n<0
    ans = NaN
end
```

The syntax is similar to a `for` loop. The first line specifies the condition we are interested in; in this case we are asking if `n` is negative. If it is, MATLAB executes the body of the statement, which is the indented sequence of statements between the `if` and the `end`.

MATLAB doesn't require you to indent the body of an `if` statement, but it makes your code more readable, so you should do it, and don't make me tell you again.

In this example, the "right" thing to do if `n` is negative is to set `ans = NaN`, which is a standard way to indicate that the result is undefined (not a number).

If the condition is not satisfied, the statements in the body are not executed. Sometimes there are alternative statements to execute when the condition is false. In that case you can extend the `if` statement with an `else` clause.

The complete version of the previous example might look like this:

```
if n<0
    ans = NaN
else
    A1 = 1;
    total = 0;
    for i=1:n
        a = A1 * 0.5^(i-1);
        total = total + a;
    end
    ans = total
end
```

Statements like `if` and `for` that contain other statements are called **compound** statements. All compound statements end with, well, `end`.

In this example, one of the statements in the `else` clause is a `for` loop. Putting one compound statement inside another is legal and common, and sometimes called **nesting**.

## 4.3   Relational operators

The operators that compare values, like `<` and `>` are called **relational operators** because they test the relationship between two values. The result of a relational operator is one of the **logical values**: either 1, which represents "true," or 0, which represents "false."

Relational operators often appear in `if` statements, but you can also evaluate them at the prompt:

```
>> x = 5;
>> x < 10
```

```
ans = 1
```

You can assign a logical value to a variable:

```
>> flag = x > 10
```

```
flag = 0
```

A variable that contains a logical value is often called a **flag** because it flags the status of some condition.

The other relational operators are `<=` and `>=`, which are self-explanatory, `==`, for "equal," and `~=`, for "not equal." (In some logic notations, the tilde is the symbol for "not.")

Don't forget that `==` is the operator that tests equality, and `=` is the assignment operator. If you try to use `=` in an `if` statement, you get a syntax error:

```
if x=5
??? if x=5
       |
Error: The expression to the left of the equals sign is not a valid
target for an assignment.
```

MATLAB thinks you are making an assignment to a variable named `if x`!

## 4.4   Logical operators

To test if a number falls in an interval, you might be tempted to write something like `0 < x < 10`, but that would be wrong, so very wrong. Unfortunately, in many cases, you will get the right answer for the wrong reason. For example:

```
>> x = 5;
>> 0 < x < 10           % right for the wrong reason
```

```
ans = 1
```

But don't be fooled!

```
>> x = 17
>> 0 < x < 10           % just plain wrong
```

```
ans = 1
```

The problem is that MATLAB is evaluating the operators from left to right, so first it checks if `0<x`. It is, so the result is 1. Then it compares the logical value 1 (not the value of `x`) to 10. Since `1<10`, the result is true, even though `x` is not in the interval.

For beginning programmers, this is an evil, evil bug!

One way around this problem is to use a nested `if` statement to check the two conditions separately:

```
ans = 0
if 0<x
    if x<10
        ans = 1
    end
end
```

But it is more concise to use the AND operator, &&, to combine the conditions.

```
>> x = 5;
>> 0<x && x<10

ans = 1

>> x = 17;
>> 0<x && x<10

ans = 0
```

The result of AND is true if *both* of the operands are true. The OR operator, ||, is true if *either or both* of the operands are true.

## 4.5   Vectors

The values we have seen so far are all single numbers, which are called **scalars** to contrast them with **vectors** and **matrices**, which are collections of numbers.

A vector in MATLAB is similar to a sequence in mathematics; it is a set of numbers that correspond to positive integers. What we called a "range" in the previous chapter was actually a vector.

In general, anything you can do with a scalar, you can also do with a vector. You can assign a vector value to a variable:

```
>> X = 1:5

X = 1    2    3    4    5
```

Variables that contain vectors are often capital letters. That's just a convention; MATLAB doesn't require it, but for beginning programmers it is a useful way to remember what is a scalar and what is a vector.

Just as with sequences, the numbers that make up the vector are called **elements**.

## 4.6   Vector arithmetic

You can perform arithmetic with vectors, too. If you add a scalar to a vector, MATLAB increments each element of the vector:

```
>> Y = X+5
```

```
Y = 6    7    8    9    10
```

The result is a new vector; the original value of X is not changed.

If you add two vectors, MATLAB adds the corresponding elements of each vector and creates a new vector that contains the sums:

```
>> Z = X+Y
```

```
Z = 7    9    11    13    15
```

But adding vectors only works if the operands are the same size. Otherwise:

```
>> W = 1:3
```

```
W = 1    2    3
```

```
>> X+W
??? Error using ==> plus
Matrix dimensions must agree.
```

The error message in this case is confusing, because we are thinking of these values as vectors, not matrices. The problem is a slight mismatch between math vocabulary and MATLAB vocabulary.

## 4.7    Everything is a matrix

In math (specifically in linear algebra) a vector is a one-dimensional sequence of values and a matrix is two-dimensional (and, if you want to think of it that way, a scalar is zero-dimensional). In MATLAB, everything is a matrix.

You can see this if you use the **whos** command to display the variables in the workspace. **whos** is similar to **who** except that it also displays the size and type of each variable.

First I'll make one of each kind of value:

```
>> scalar = 5
```

```
scalar = 5
```

```
>> vector = 1:5
```

```
vector = 1    2    3    4    5
```

```
>> matrix = ones(2,3)
```

```
matrix =

    1    1    1
    1    1    1
```

ones is a function that builds a new matrix with the given number of rows and columns, and sets all the elements to 1. Now let's see what we've got.

```
>> whos
   Name       Size                Bytes  Class

   scalar     1x1                     8  double array
   vector     1x5                    40  double array
   matrix     2x3                    32  double array
```

According to MATLAB, everything is a double array: "double" is another name for double-precision floating-point numbers, and "array" is another name for a matrix.

The only difference is the size, which is specified by the number of rows and columns. The thing we called scalar is, according to MATLAB, a matrix with one row and one column. Our vector is really a matrix with one row and 5 columns. And, of course, matrix is a matrix.

The point of all this is that you can think of your values as scalars, vectors, and matrices, and I think you should, as long as you remember that MATLAB thinks everything is a matrix.

Here's another example where the error message only makes sense if you know what is happening under the hood:

```
>> X = 1:5

X = 1     2     3     4     5

>> Y = 1:5

Y = 1     2     3     4     5

>> Z = X*Y
??? Error using ==> mtimes
Inner matrix dimensions must agree.
```

First of all, mtimes is the MATLAB function that performs matrix multiplication. The reason the "inner matrix dimensions must agree" is that the way matrix multiplication is defined in linear algebra, the number of rows in X has to equal the number of columns in Y (those are the inner dimensions).

If you don't know linear algebra, this doesn't make much sense. When you saw X*Y you probably expected it to multiply each the the elements of X by the corresponding element of Y and put the results into a new vector. That operation is called **elementwise** multiplication, and the operator that performs it is .*:

```
>> X .* Y

ans = 1     4     9     16     25
```

We'll get back to the elementwise operators later; you can forget about them for now.

## 4.8 Indices

You can select elements of a vector with parentheses:

```
>> Y = 6:10

Y = 6      7      8      9      10

>> Y(1)

ans = 6

>> Y(5)

ans = 10
```

This means that the first element of Y is 6 and the fifth element is 10. The number in parentheses is called the **index** because it indicates which element of the vector you want.

The index can be any kind of expression.

```
>> i = 1;

>> Y(i+1)

ans = 7
```

Loops and vectors go together like the storm and rain. For example, this loop displays the elements of Y.

```
for i=1:5
    Y(i)
end
```

Each time through the loop we use a different value of i as an index into Y.

A limitation of this example is that we had to know the number of elements in Y. We can make it more general by using the **length** function, which returns the number of elements in a vector:

```
for i=1:length(Y)
    Y(i)
end
```

There. Now that will work for a vector of any length.

## 4.9 Indexing errors

An index can be any kind of expression, but the value of the expression has to be a positive integer, and it has to be less than or equal to the length of the vector. If it's zero or negative, you get this:

```
>> Y(0)
??? Subscript indices must either be real positive integers or
logicals.
```

"Subscript indices" is MATLAB's longfangled way to say "indices." "Real positive integers" means that complex numbers are out. And you can forget about "logicals" for now.

If the index is too big, you get this:

```
>> Y(6)
??? Index exceeds matrix dimensions.
```

There's the "m" word again, but other than that, this message is pretty clear.

Finally, don't forget that the index has to be an integer:

```
>> Y(1.5)
??? Subscript indices must either be real positive integers or
logicals.
```

## 4.10   Vectors and sequences

Vectors and sequences go together like ice cream and apple pie. For example, another way to evaluate the Fibonacci sequence is by storing successive values in a vector. Again, the definition of the Fibonacci sequence is $F_1 = 1$, $F_2 = 1$, and $F_i = F_{i-1} + F_{i-2}$ for $i \geq 3$. In MATLAB, that looks like

```
F(1) = 1
F(2) = 1
for i=3:n
    F(i) = F(i-1) + F(i-2)
end
ans = F(n)
```
*indices are similar to* $F(x)$

Notice that I am using a capital letter for the vector F and lower-case letters for the scalars i and n. At the end, the script extracts the final element of F and stores it in ans, since the result of this script is supposed to be the $n$th Fibonacci number, not the whole sequence.

If you had any trouble with Exercise 3.5, you have to appreciate the simplicity of this version. The MATLAB syntax is similar to the math notation, which makes it easier to check correctness. The only drawbacks are

- You have to be careful with the range of the loop. In this version, the loop runs from 3 to n, and each time we assign a value to the ith element. It would also work to "shift" the index over by two, running the loop from 1 to n-2:

```
F(1) = 1
F(2) = 1
for i=1:n-2
    F(i+2) = F(i+1) + F(i)
end
ans = F(n)
```

Either version is fine, but you have to choose one approach and be consistent. If you combine elements of both, you will get confused. I prefer the version that has `F(i)` on the left side of the assignment, so that each time through the loop it assigns the ith element.

- If you really only want the $n$th Fibonacci number, then storing the whole sequence wastes some storage space. But if wasting space makes your code easier to write and debug, that's probably ok.

**Exercise 4.1** *Write a loop that computes the first* **n** *elements of the geometric sequence* $A_{i+1} = A_i/2$ *with* $A_1 = 1$. *Notice that the math notation puts* $A_{i+1}$ *on the left side of the equality. When you translate to MATLAB, you may want to shift the index.*

## 4.11 Plotting vectors

Plotting and vectors go together like the moon and June, whatever that means. If you call `plot` with a single vector as an argument, MATLAB plots the indices on the $x$-axis and the elements on the $y$-axis. To plot the Fibonacci numbers we computed in the previous section:

```
plot(F)
```

This display is often useful for debugging, especially if your vectors are big enough that displaying the elements on the screen is unwieldy.

If you call `plot` with two vectors as arguments, MATLAB plots the second one as a function of the first; that is, it treats the first vector as a sequence of $x$ values and the second as corresponding $y$ value and plots a sequence of $(x, y)$ points.

```
X = 1:5
Y = 6:10
plot(X, Y)
```

By default, MATLAB draws a blue line, but you can override that setting with the same kind of string we saw in Section 3.5. For example, the string `'ro-'` tells MATLAB to plot a red circle at each data point; the hyphen means the points should be connected with a line.

In this example, I stuck with the convention of naming the first argument `X` (since it is plotted on the $x$-axis) and the second `Y`. There is nothing special about these names; you could just as well plot `X` as a function of `Y`. MATLAB always treats the first vector as the "independent" variable, and the second as the "dependent" variable (if those terms are familiar to you).

## 4.12 Reduce

A frequent use of loops is to run through the elements of an array and add them up, or multiply them together, or compute the sum of their squares, etc. This kind of operation is called **reduce**, because it reduces a vector with multiple elements down to a single scalar.

For example, this loop adds up the elements of a vector named X (which we assume has been defined).

```
total = 0
for i=1:length(X)
    total = total + X(i)
end
ans = total
```

The use of `total` as an accumulator is similar to what we saw in Section 3.7. Again, we use the `length` function to find the upper bound of the range, so this loop will work regardless of the length of X. Each time through the loop, we add in the ith element of X, so at the end of the loop `total` contains the sum of the elements.

**Exercise 4.2** *Write a similar loop that multiplies all the elements of a vector together. You might want to call the accumulator* `product`, *and you might want to think about the initial value you give it before the loop.*

## 4.13   Apply

Another common use of a loop is to run through the elements of a vector, perform some operation on the elements, and create a new vector with the results. This kind of operation is called **apply**, because you apply the operation to each element in the vector.

For example, the following loop computes a vector Y that contains the squares of the elements of X (assuming, again, that X is already defined).

```
for i=1:length(X)
    Y(i) = X(i)^2
end
```

**Exercise 4.3** *Write a loop that computes a vector Y that contains the sines of the elements of* X. *To test your loop, write a script that*

1. *Uses* `linspace` *(see the documentation) to assign to* X *a vector with 100 elements running from 0 to* $2\pi$.

2. *Uses your loop to store the sines in* Y.

3. *Plots the elements of* Y *as a function of the elements of* X.

## 4.14   Search

Yet another use of loops is to search the elements of a vector and return the index of the value you are looking for (or the first value that has a particular property). For example, if a vector contains the computed altitude of a falling object, you might want to know the index where the object touches down (assuming that the ground is at altitude 0).

To create some fake data, we'll use an extended version of the colon operator:

```
X = 10:-1:-10
```

The values in this range run from 10 to -10, with a **step size** of -1. The step size is the interval between elements of the range.

The following loop finds the index of the element 0 in X:

```
for i=1:length(X)
    if X(i) == 0
        ans = i
    end
end
```

One funny thing about this loop is that it keeps going after it finds what it is looking for. That might be what you want; if the target value appears more than one, this loop provides the index of the *last* one.

But if you want the index of the first one (or you know that there is only one), you can save some unnecessary looping by using the **break** statement.

```
for i=1:length(X)
    if X(i) == 0
        ans = i
        break
    end
end
```

**break** does pretty much what it sounds like. It ends the loop and proceeds immediately to the next statement after the loop (in this case, there isn't one, so the script ends).

This example demonstrates the basic idea of a search, but it also demonstrates a dangerous use of the if statement. Remember that floating-point values are often only approximately right. That means that if you look for a perfect match, you might not find it. For example, try this:

```
X = linspace(1,2)
for i=1:length(X)
    Y(i) = sin(X(i))
end
plot(X, Y)
```

You can see in the plot that the value of $\sin x$ goes through 0.9 in this range, but if you search for the index where Y(i) == 0.9, you will come up empty.

```
for i=1:length(Y)
    if Y(i) == 0.9
        ans = i
        break
    end
end
```

The condition is never true, so the body of the if statement is never executed.

Even though the plot shows a continuous line, don't forget that X and Y are sequences of discrete (and usually approximate) values. As a rule, you should (almost) never use the == operator to compare floating-point values. There are a number of ways to get around this limitation; we will get to them later.

**Exercise 4.4**  *Write a loop that finds the index of the first negative number in a vector and stores it in* ans. *If there are no negative numbers, it should set* ans *to -1 (which is not a legal index, so it is a good way to indicate the special case).*

## 4.15   Spoiling the fun

Experienced MATLAB programmers would never write the kind of loops in this chapter, because MATLAB provides simpler and faster ways to perform many reduce, filter and search operations.

For example, the `sum` function computes the sum of the elements in a vector and `prod` computes the product.

Many apply operations can be done with elementwise operators. The following statement is more concise than the loop in Section 4.13

```
Y = X .^ 2
```

Also, most built-in MATLAB functions work with vectors:

```
X = linspace(0, 2*pi)
Y = sin(X)
plot(X, Y)
```

Finally, the `find` function can perform search operations, but understanding it requires a couple of concepts we haven't got to, so for now you are better off on your own.

I started with simple loops because I wanted to demonstrate the basic concepts and give you a chance to practice. At some point you will probably have to write a loop for which there is no MATLAB shortcut, but you have to work your way up from somewhere.

If you understand loops and you are are comfortable with the shortcuts, feel free to use them! Otherwise, you can always write out the loop.

**Exercise 4.5**  *Write an expression that computes the sum of the squares of the elements of a vector.*

## 4.16   Glossary

**compound:** A statement, like `if` and `for`, that contains other statements in an indented body.

**nesting:** Putting one compound statement in the body of another.

**relational operator:** An operator that compares two values and generates a logical value as a result.

**logical value:** A value that represents either "true" or "false". MATLAB uses the values 1 and 0, respectively.

**flag:** A variable that contains a logical value, often used to store the status of some condition.

**scalar:** A single value.

**vector:** A sequence of values.

**matrix:** A two-dimensional collection of values (also called "array" in some MATLAB documentation).

**index:** An integer value used to indicate one of the values in a vector or matrix (also called subscript in some MATLAB documentation).

**element:** One of the values in a vector or matrix.

**elementwise:** An operation that acts on the individual elements of a vector or matrix (unlike some linear algebra operations).

**reduce:** A way of processing the elements of a vector and generating a single value; for example, the sum of the elements.

**apply:** A way of processing a vector by performing some operation on each of the elements, producing a vector that contains the results.

**search:** A way of processing a vector by examining the elements in order until one is found that has the desired property.

## 4.17 Exercises

**Exercise 4.6** *The ratio of consecutive Fibonacci numbers, $F_{n+1}/F_n$, converges to a constant value as n increases. Write a script that computes a vector with the first n elements of a Fibonacci sequence (assuming that the variable* n *is defined), and then computes a new vector that contains the ratios of consecutive Fibonacci numbers. Plot this vector to see if it seems to converge. What value does it converge on?*

**Exercise 4.7** *A certain famous system of differential equations can be approximated by a system of difference equations that looks like this:*

$$x_{i+1} = x_i + \sigma \left( y_i - x_i \right) dt \tag{4.1}$$
$$y_{i+1} = y_i + \left[ x_i (r - z_i) - y_i \right] dt \tag{4.2}$$
$$z_{i+1} = z_i + \left( x_i y_i - b z_i \right) dt \tag{4.3}$$

- *Write a script that computes the first 10 elements of the sequences X, Y and Z and stores them in vectors named* X, Y *and* Z.

  *Use the initial values $X_1 = 1$, $Y_1 = 2$ and $Z_1 = 3$, with values $\sigma = 10$, $b = 8/3$ and $r = 28$, and with time step $dt = 0.01$.*

- *Read the documentation for* plot3 *and* comet3 *and plot the results in 3 dimensions.*

- *Once the code is working, use semi-colons to suppress the output and then run the program with sequence length 100, 1000 and 10000.*

- *Run the program again with different starting conditions. What effect does it have on the result?*

- *Run the program with different values for $\sigma$, $b$ and $r$ and see if you can get a sense of how each variable affects the system.*

**Exercise 4.8** *The logistic map is often cited as an example of how complex, chaotic behaviour can arise from simple non-linear dynamical equations [some of this description is adapted from the Wikipedia page on the logistic map]. It was popularized in a seminal 1976 paper by the biologist Robert May.*

*It has been used to model the biomass of a species in the presence of limiting factors such as food supply and disease. In this case, there are two processes at work: (1) A reproductive process increases the biomass of the species in proportion to the current population. (2) A starvation process causes the biomass to decrease at a rate proportional to the carrying capacity of the environment less the current population.*

*Mathematically this can be written as*

$$X_{i+1} = rX_i(1 - X_i)$$

*where $X_i$ is a number between zero and one that represents the biomass at year $i$, and $r$ is a positive number that represents a combined rate for reproduction and starvation.*

- *Write a script named* `logmap` *that computes the first 50 elements of $X$ with* `r=3.9` *and* `X1=0.5`*, where* `r` *is the parameter of the logistic map and* `X1` *is the initial population.*

- *Plot the results for a range of values of $r$ from 2.4 to 4.0. How does the behavior of the system change as you vary $r$.*

- *One way to characterize the effect of $r$ is to make a plot with $r$ on the x-axis and biomass on the y axis, and to show, for each value of $r$, the values of biomass that occur in steady state. See if you can figure out how to generate this plot.*

# Chapter 5

# Functions

## 5.1 Name Collisions

Remember that all of your scripts run in the same workspace, so if one script changes the value of a variable, all your other scripts see the change. With a small number of simple scripts, that's not a problem, but eventually the interactions between scripts become unmanageable.

For example, the following (increasingly familiar) script computes the sum of the first n terms in a geometric sequence, but it also has the **side-effect** of assigning values to A1, total, i and a.

```
A1 = 1;
total = 0;
for i=1:10
    a = A1 * 0.5^(i-1);
    total = total + a;
end
ans = total
```

If you were using any of those variable names before calling this script, you might be surprised to find, after running the script, that their values had changed. If you have two scripts that use the same variable names, you might find that they work separately and then break when you try to combine them. This kind of interaction is called a **name collision**.

As the number of scripts you write increases, and they get longer and more complex, name collisions become more of a problem. Avoiding this problem is one of the motivations for functions.

## 5.2 Functions

A **function** is like a script, except

- Each function has its own workspace, so any variables defined inside a function only exist while the function is running, and don't interfere with variables in other workspaces, even if they have the same name.

- Function inputs and outputs are defined carefully to avoid unexpected interactions.

To define a new function, you create an M-file with the name you want, and put a function definition in it. For example, to create a function named `myfunc`, create an M-file named `myfunc.m` and put the following definition into it.

```
function res = myfunc(x)
    s = sin(x)
    c = cos(x)
    res = abs(s) + abs(c)
end
```

The first word of the file has to be the word `function`, because that's how MATLAB tells the difference between a script and a function file.

A function definition is a compound statement. The first line is called the **signature** of the function; it defines the inputs and outputs of the function. In this case the **input variable** is named `x`. When this function is called, the argument provided by the user will be assigned to `x`.

The **output variable** is named `res`, which is short for "result." You can call the output variable whatever you want, but as a convention, I like to call it `res`. Usually the last thing a function does is assign a value to the output variable.

Once you have defined a new function, you call it the same way you call built-in MATLAB functions. If you call the function as a statement, MATLAB puts the result into `ans`:

```
>> myfunc(1)

s = 0.84147098480790

c = 0.54030230586814

res = 1.38177329067604

ans = 1.38177329067604
```

But it is more common (and better style) to assign the result to a variable:

```
>> y = myfunc(1)

s = 0.84147098480790

c = 0.54030230586814

res = 1.38177329067604

y = 1.38177329067604
```

While you are debugging a new function, you might want to display intermediate results like this, but once it is working, you will want to add semi-colons to make it a **silent function**. Most built-in functions are silent; they compute a result, but they don't display anything (except sometimes warning messages).

Each function has its own workspace, which is created when the function starts and destroyed when the function ends. If you try to access (read or write) the variables defined inside a function, you will find that they don't exist.

```
>> clear
>> y = myfunc(1);
>> who

Your variables are: y

>> s
??? Undefined function or variable 's'.
```

The only value from the function that you can access is the result, which in this case is assigned to y.

If you have variables named s or c in your workspace before you call myfunc, they will still be there when the function completes.

```
>> s = 1;
>> c = 1;
>> y = myfunc(1);
>> s, c

s = 1
c = 1
```

So inside a function you can use whatever variable names you want without worrying about collisions.

## 5.3 Documentation

At the beginning of every function file, you should include a comment that explains what the function does.

```
% res = myfunc (x)
% Compute the Manhattan distance from the origin to the
% point on the unit circle with angle (x) in radians.

function res = myfunc (x)
    s = sin(x);
    c = cos(x);
    res = abs(s) + abs(c);
end
```

When you ask for **help**, MATLAB prints the comment you provide.

```
>> help myfunc
  res = myfunc (x)
  Compute the Manhattan distance from the origin to the
  point on the unit circle with angle (x) in radians.
```

There are lots of conventions about what should be included in these comments. Among other things, it is a good idea to include

- The signature of the function, which includes the name of the function, the input variable(s) and the output variable(s).

- A clear, concise, abstract description of what the function does. An **abstract** description is one that leaves out the details of *how* the function works, and includes only information that someone using the function needs to know. You can put additional comments inside the function that explain the details.

- An explanation of what the input variables mean; for example, in this case it is important to note that x is considered to be an angle in radians.

- Any preconditions and postconditions.

## 5.4  Function names

There are two "gotchas" that come up when you start naming functions. The first is that the "real" name of your function is determined by the file name, *not* by the name you put in the function signature. As a matter of style, you should make sure that they are always the same, but if you make a mistake, or if you change the name of a function, it is easy to get confused.

In the spirit of making errors on purpose, change the name of the function in myfunc to something_else, and then run it again.

If this is what you put in myfunc.m:

```
function res = something_else (x)
    s = sin(x);
    c = cos(x);
    res = abs(s) + abs(c);
end
```

Then here's what you'll get:

```
>> y = myfunc(1);
>> y = something_else(1);
??? Undefined command/function 'something_else'.
```

The other gotcha is that your function names can collide with built-in MATLAB functions. For example, if you create an M-file named sum.m, and then call sum, MATLAB might call *your* new function, not the built-in version! Which one actually gets called depends on the order of the directories in the search path, and (in some cases) on the arguments. As an example, put the following code in a file named sum.m:

```
function res = sum(x)
    res = 7;
end
```

And then try this:

```
>> sum(1:3)

ans = 6

>> sum

ans = 7
```

In the first case MATLAB used the built-in function; in the second case it ran your function! This kind of interaction can be very confusing. Before you create a new function, check to see if there is already a MATLAB function with the same name. If there is, choose another name!


## 5.5   Multiple input variables

Functions can, and often do, take more than one input variable. For example, the following function takes two input variables, a and b:

```
function res = hypotenuse(a, b)
    res = sqrt(a^2 + b^2);
end
```

If you remember the Pythagorean Theorem, you probably figured out that this function computes the length of the hypotenuse of a right triangle if the lengths of the adjacent sides are a and b. (There is a MATLAB function called hypot that does the same thing.)

If we call it from the Command Window with arguments 3 and 4, we can confirm that the length of the third side is 5.

```
>> c = hypotenuse(3, 4)

c = 5
```

The arguments you provide are assigned to the input variables in order, so in this case 3 is assigned to a and 4 is assigned to b. MATLAB checks that you provide the right number of arguments; if you provide too few, you get

```
>> c = hypotenuse(3)
??? Input argument "b" is undefined.

Error in ==> hypotenuse at 2
    res = sqrt(a^2 + b^2);
```

This error message is confusing, because it suggests that the problem is in hypotenuse rather than in the function call. Keep that in mind when you are debugging.

If you provide too many arguments, you get

```
>> c = hypotenuse(3, 4, 5)
??? Error using ==> hypotenuse
Too many input arguments.
```

Which is a better message.

## 5.6   Logical functions

In Section 4.4 we used logical operators to compare values. MATLAB also provides **logical functions** that check for certain conditions and return logical values: 1 for "true" and 0 for "false".

For example, `isprime` checks to see whether a number is prime.

```
>> isprime(17)

ans = 1

>> isprime(21)

ans = 0
```

The functions `isscalar` and `isvector` check whether a value is a scalar or vector; if both are false, you can assume it is a matrix (at least for now).

To check whether a value you have computed is an integer, you might be tempted to use `isinteger`. But that would be wrong, so very wrong. `isinteger` checks whether a value belongs to one of the integer types (a topic we have not discussed); it doesn't check whether a floating-point value happens to be integral.

```
>> c = hypotenuse(3, 4)

c = 5

>> isinteger(c)

ans = 0
```

To do that, we have to write our own logical function, which we'll call `isintegral`:

```
function res = isintegral(x)
    if round(x) == x
        res = 1;
    else
        res = 0;
    end
end
```

This function is good enough for most applications, but remember that floating-point values are only approximately right; in some cases the approximation is an integer but the actual value is not.

## 5.7   An incremental development example

Let's say that we want to write a program to search for "Pythagorean triples:" sets of integral values, like 3, 4 and 5, that are the lengths of the sides of a right triangle. In other words, we would like to find integral values $a$, $b$ and $c$ such that $a^2 + b^2 = c^2$.

Here are the steps we will follow to develop the program incrementally.

- Write a script named `find_triples` and start with a simple statement like x=5.

- Write a loop that enumerates values of $a$ from 1 to 3, and displays them.

- Write a nested loop that enumerates values of $b$ from 1 to 4, and displays them.

- Inside the loop, call `hypotenuse` to compute $c$ and display it.

- Use `isintegral` to check whether $c$ is an integral value.

- Use an if statement to print only the triples $a$, $b$ and $c$ that pass the test.

- Transform the script into a function.

- Generalize the function to take input variables that specify the range to search.

So the first draft of this program is x=5, which might seem silly, but if you start simple and add a little bit at a time, you will avoid a lot of debugging.

Here's the second draft:

```
for a=1:3
    a
end
```

At each step, the program is testable: it produces output (or another visible effect) that you can check.

## 5.8   Nested loops

The third draft contains a nested loop:

```
for a=1:3
    a
    for b=1:4
        b
    end
end
```

The inner loop gets executed 3 times, once for each value of a, so here's what the output looks like (I adjusted the spacing to make the structure clear):

```
>> find_triples

a = 1    b = 1
         b = 2
         b = 3
         b = 4

a = 2    b = 1
         b = 2
         b = 3
         b = 4

a = 3    b = 1
         b = 2
         b = 3
         b = 4
```

The next step is to compute $c$ for each pair of values $a$ and $b$.

```
for a=1:3
    for b=1:4
        c = hypotenuse(a, b);
        [a, b, c]
    end
end
```

To display the values of a, b and c, I am using a feature we haven't seen before. The bracket operator creates a new matrix which, when it is displayed, shows the three values on one line:

```
>> find_triples

ans = 1.0000    1.0000    1.4142
ans = 1.0000    2.0000    2.2361
ans = 1.0000    3.0000    3.1623
ans = 1.0000    4.0000    4.1231
ans = 2.0000    1.0000    2.2361
ans = 2.0000    2.0000    2.8284
ans = 2.0000    3.0000    3.6056
ans = 2.0000    4.0000    4.4721
ans = 3.0000    1.0000    3.1623
ans = 3.0000    2.0000    3.6056
ans = 3.0000    3.0000    4.2426
ans = 3         4         5
```

Sharp-eyed readers will notice that we are wasting some effort here. After checking $a = 1$ and $b = 2$, there is no point in checking $a = 2$ and $b = 1$. We can eliminate the extra work by adjusting the range of the second loop:

```
for a=1:3
    for b=a:4
        c = hypotenuse(a, b);
```

```
        [a, b, c]
    end
end
```

If you are following along, run this version to make sure it has the expected effect.

## 5.9   Conditions and flags

The next step is to check for integral values of $c$. This loop calls isintegral and prints the resulting logical value.

```
for a=1:3
    for b=a:4
        c = hypotenuse(a, b);
        flag = isintegral(c);
        [c, flag]
    end
end
```

By not displaying a and b I made it easy to scan the output to make sure that the values of c and flag look right.

```
>> find_triples
```

```
ans = 1.4142        0
ans = 2.2361        0
ans = 3.1623        0
ans = 4.1231        0
ans = 2.8284        0
ans = 3.6056        0
ans = 4.4721        0
ans = 4.2426        0
ans = 5             1
```

I chose the ranges for a and b to be small (so the amount of output is manageable), but to contain at least one Pythagorean triple. A constant challenge of debugging is to generate enough output to demonstrate that the code is working (or not) without being overwhelmed.

The next step is to use flag to display only the successful triples:

```
for a=1:3
    for b=a:4
        c = hypotenuse(a, b);
        flag = isintegral(c);
        if flag
            [a, b, c]
        end
    end
end
```

Now the output is elegant and simple:

```
>> find_triples
```

```
ans = 3    4    5
```

## 5.10   Encapsulation and generalization

As a script, this program has the side-effect of assigning values to a, b, c and flag, which would make it hard to use if any of those names were in use. By wrapping the code in a function, we can avoid name collisions; this process is called **encapsulation** because it isolates this program from the workspace.

In order to put the code we have written inside a function, we have to indent the whole thing. The MATLAB editor provides a shortcut for doing that, the Increase Indent command under the Text menu. Just don't forget to unselect the text before you start typing!

The first draft of the function takes no input variables:

```
function res = find_triples ()
    for a=1:3
        for b=a:4
            c = hypotenuse(a, b);
            flag = isintegral(c);
            if flag
                [a, b, c]
            end
        end
    end
end
```

The empty parentheses in the signature are not strictly necessary, but they make it apparent that there are no input variables. Similarly, when I call the new function, I like to use parentheses to remind me that it is a function, not a script:

```
>> find_triples()
```

The output variable isn't strictly necessary, either; it never gets assigned a value. But I put it there as a matter of habit, and also so my function signatures all have the same structure.

The next step is to generalize this function by adding input variables. The natural generalization is to replace the constant values 3 and 4 with a variable so we can search an arbitrarily large range of values.

```
function res = find_triples (n)
    for a=1:n
        for b=a:n
            c = hypotenuse(a, b);
            flag = isintegral(c);
            if flag
                [a, b, c]
            end
```

```
        end
    end
end
```

Here are the results for the range from 1 to 15:

```
>> find_triples(15)

ans = 3     4     5
ans = 5    12    13
ans = 6     8    10
ans = 8    15    17
ans = 9    12    15
```

Some of these are more interesting than others. The triples $5, 12, 13$ and $8, 15, 17$ are "new," but the others are just multiples of the $3, 4, 5$ triangle we already knew.

## 5.11   A misstep

When you change the signature of a function, you have to change all the places that call the function, too. For example, suppose I decided to add a third input variable to hypotenuse:

```
function res = hypotenuse(a, b, d)
    res = (a.^d + b.^d) ^ (1/d);
end
```

When d is 2, this does the same thing it did before. There is no practical reason to generalize the function in this way; it's just an example. Now when you run find_triples, you get:

```
>> find_triples(20)
??? Input argument "d" is undefined.

Error in ==> hypotenuse at 2
    res = (a.^d + b.^d) ^ (1/d);

Error in ==> find_triples at 7
            c = hypotenuse(a, b);
```

So that makes it pretty easy to find the error. This is an example of a development technique that is sometimes useful: rather than search the program for all the places that use hypotenuse, you can run the program and use the error messages to guide you.

But this technique is risky, especially if the error messages make suggestions about what to change. If you do what you're told, you might make the error message go away, but that doesn't mean the program will do the right thing. MATLAB doesn't know what the program is *supposed* to do, but you should.

And that brings us to the Eighth Theorem of debugging:

> Error messages sometimes tell you what's wrong, but they seldom tell you what to do (and when they try, they're usually wrong).

## 5.12   continue

As one final improvement, let's modify the function so that it only displays the "lowest" of each Pythagorean triple, and not the multiples.

The simplest way to eliminate the multiples is to check whether $a$ and $b$ share a common factor. If they do, then dividing both by the common factor yields a smaller, similar triangle that has already been checked.

MATLAB provides a `gcd` function that computes the greatest common divisor of two numbers. If the result is greater than 1, then $a$ and $b$ share a common factor and we can use the `continue` statement to skip to the next pair:

```
function res = find_triples (n)
    for a=1:n
        for b=a:n
            if gcd(a,b) > 1
                continue
            end
            c = hypotenuse(a, b);
            if isintegral(c)
                [a, b, c]
            end
        end
    end
end
```

`continue` causes the program to end the current iteration immediately (without executing the rest of the body), jump to the top of the loop, and "continue" with the next iteration.

In this case, since there are two loops, it might not be obvious which loop to jump to, but the rule is to jump to the inner-most loop (which is what we wanted).

I also simplified the program slightly by eliminating `flag` and using `isintegral` as the condition of the `if` statement.

Here are the results with n=40:

```
>> find_triples(40)

ans =    3     4     5
ans =    5    12    13
ans =    7    24    25
ans =    8    15    17
ans =    9    40    41
ans =   12    35    37
ans =   20    21    29
```

There is an interesting connection between Fibonacci numbers and Pythagorean triples. If $F$ is a Fibonacci sequence, then

$$(F_n F_{n+3}, 2F_{n+1}F_{n+2}, F_{n+1}^2 + F_{n+2}^2)$$

is a Pythagorean triple for all $n \geq 1$.

**Exercise 5.1**  *Write a function named* `fib_triple` *that takes an input variable* n, *uses* `fibonacci2` *to compute the first* n *Fibonacci numbers, and then checks whether this formula produces a Pythagorean triple for each number in the sequence.*

## 5.13   Mechanism and leap of faith

Let's review the sequence of steps that occur when you call a function:

1. Before the function starts running, MATLAB creates a new workspace for it.

2. MATLAB evaluates each of the arguments and assigns the resulting values, in order, to the input variables (which live in the *new* workspace).

3. The body of the code executes. Somewhere in the body (often the last line) a value gets assigned to the output variable.

4. The function's workspace is destroyed; the only thing that remains is the value of the output variable and any side effects the function had (like displaying values or creating a figure).

5. The program resumes from where it left off. The value of the function call is the value of the output variable.

When you are reading a program and you come to a function call, there are two ways to interpret it:

- You can think about the mechanism I just described, and follow the execution of the program into the function and back, or

- You can take the "leap of faith": assume that the function works correctly, and go on to the next statement after the function call.

When you use built-in functions, it is natural to take the leap of faith, in part because you expect that most MATLAB functions work, and in part because you don't generally have access to the code in the body of the function.

But when you start writing your own functions, you will probably find yourself following the "flow of execution." This can be useful while you are learning, but as you gain experience, you should get more comfortable with the idea of writing a function, testing it to make sure it works, and then forgetting about the details of how it works.

Forgetting about details is called **abstraction**; in the context of functions, abstraction means forgetting about *how* a function works, and just assuming (after appropriate testing) that it works.

## 5.14    Glossary

**side-effect:** An effect, like modifying the workspace, that is not the primary purpose of a script.

**name collision:** The scenario where two scripts that use the same variable name interfere with each other.

**input variable:** A variable in a function that gets its value, when the function is called, from one of the arguments.

**output variable:** A variable in a function that is used to return a value from the function to the caller.

**signature:** The first line of a function definition, which specifies the names of the function, the input variables and the output variables.

**silent function:** A function that doesn't display anything or generate a figure, or have any other side-effects.

**logical function:** A function that returns a logical value (1 for "true" or 0 for "false").

**encapsulation:** The process of wrapping part of a program in a function in order to limit interactions (including name collisions) between the function and the rest of the program.

**generalization:** Making a function more versatile by replacing specific values with input variables.

**abstraction:** The process of ignoring the details of how a function works in order to focus on a simpler model of what the function does.

## 5.15    Exercises

**Exercise 5.2** *Take any of the scripts you have written so far, encapsulate the code in an appropriately-named function, and generalize the function by adding one or more input variables.*

*Make the function silent and then call it from the Command Window and confirm that you can display the output value.*

# Chapter 6

# Zero-finding

## 6.1  Why functions?

The previous chapter explained some of the benefits of functions, including

- Each function has its own workspace, so using functions helps avoid name collisions.

- Functions lend themselves to incremental development: you can debug the body of the function first (as a script), then encapsulate it as a function, and then generalize it by adding input variables.

- Functions allow you to divide a large problem into small pieces, work on the pieces one at a time, and then assemble a complete solution.

- Once you have a function working, you can forget about the details of how it works and concentrate on what it does. This process of abstraction is an important tool for managing the complexity of large programs.

Another reason you should consider using functions is that many of the tools provided by MATLAB require you to write functions. For example, in this chapter we will use `fzero` to find solutions of nonlinear equations. Later we will use `ode45` to approximate solutions to differential equations.

## 6.2  Maps

In mathematics, a **map** is a correspondence between one set called the **range** and another set called the **domain**. For each element of the range, the map specifies the corresponding element of the domain.

You can think of a sequence as a map from positive integers to elements. You can think of a vector as a map from indices to elements. In these cases the maps are **discrete** because the elements of the range are countable.

You can also think of a function as a map from inputs to outputs, but in this case the range is **continuous** because the inputs can take any value, not just integers. (Strictly speaking, the set of floating-point numbers is discrete, but since floating-point numbers are meant to represent real numbers, we think of them as continuous.)

## 6.3   A note on notation

In this chapter I need to start talking about mathematical functions, and I am going to use a notation you might not have seen before.

If you have studied functions in a math class, you have probably seen something like

$$f(x) = x^2 - 2x - 3$$

which is supposed to mean that $f$ is a function that maps from $x$ to $x^2 - 2x - 3$. The problem is that $f(x)$ is also used to mean the value of $f$ that corresponds to a particular value of $x$. So I don't like this notation. I prefer

$$f : x \to x^2 - 2x - 3$$

which means "f is the function that maps from $x$ to $x^2 - 2x - 3$." In MATLAB, this would be expressed like this:

```
function res = error_func(x)
    res = x^2 - 2*x -3;
end
```

I'll explain soon why this function is called **error_func**. Now, back to our regularly-scheduled programming.

## 6.4   Nonlinear equations

What does it mean to "solve" an equation? That may seem like an obvious question, but I want to take a minute to think about it, starting with a simple example: let's say that we want to know the value of a variable, $x$, but all we know about it is the relationship $x^2 = a$.

If you have taken algebra, you probably know how to "solve" this equation: you take the square root of both sides and get $x = \sqrt{a}$. Then, with the satisfaction of a job well done, you move on to the next problem.

But what have you really done? The relationship you derived is equivalent to the relationship you started with—they contain the same information about $x$—so why is the second one preferable to the first?

There are two reasons. One is that the relationship is now "explicit in $x$;" because $x$ is all alone on the left side, we can treat the right side as a recipe for computing $x$, assuming that we know the value of $a$.

The other reason is that the recipe is written in terms of operations we know how to perform. Assuming that we know how to compute square roots, we can compute the value of $x$ for any value of $a$.

When people talk about solving an equation, what they usually mean is something like "finding an equivalent relationship that is explicit in one of the variables." In the context of this book, that's what I will call an **analytic solution**, to distinguish it from a **numerical solution**, which is what we are going to do next.

To demonstrate a numerical solution, consider the equation $x^2 - 2x = 3$. You could solve this analytically, either by factoring it or by using the quadratic equation, and you would discover that there are two solutions, $x = 3$ and $x = -1$. Alternatively, you could solve it numerically by rewriting it as $x = \sqrt{2x + 3}$.

This equation is not explicit, since $x$ appears on both sides, so it is not clear that this move did any good at all. But suppose that we had some reason to expect there to be a solution near 4. We could start with $x = 4$ as an "initial guess," and then use the equation $x = \sqrt{2x + 3}$ iteratively to compute successive approximations of the solution.

Here's what would happen:

```
>> x = 4;

>> x = sqrt(2*x+3)

x = 3.3166

>> x = sqrt(2*x+3)

x = 3.1037

>> x = sqrt(2*x+3)

x = 3.0344

>> x = sqrt(2*x+3)

x = 3.0114

>> x = sqrt(2*x+3)

x = 3.0038
```

After each iteration, x is closer to the correct answer, and after 5 iterations, the relative error is about 0.1%, which is good enough for most purposes.

Techniques that generate numerical solutions are called **numerical methods**. The nice thing about the method I just demonstrated is that it is simple, but it doesn't always work as well as it did in this example, and it is not used very often in practice. We'll see one of the more practical alternatives in a minute.

## 6.5   Zero-finding

A nonlinear equation like $x^2 - 2x = 3$ is a statement of equality that is true for some values of $x$ and false for others. A value that makes it true is a solution; any other value is a non-solution. But for any given non-solution, there is no sense of whether it is close or far from a solution, or where we might look to find one.

To address this limitation, it is useful to rewrite non-linear equations as zero-finding problems:

- The first step is to define an "error function" that computes how far a given value of $x$ is from being a solution.

  In this example, the error function is

  $$f : x \rightarrow x^2 - 2x - 3$$

  Any value of $x$ that makes $f(x) = 0$ is also a solution of the original equation.

- The next step is to find values of $x$ that make $f(x) = 0$. These values are called **zeros of the function**, or sometimes roots.

Zero-finding lends itself to numerical solution because we can use the values of $f$, evaluated at various values of $x$, to make reasonable inferences about where to look for zeros.

For example, if we can find two values $x_1$ and $x_2$ such that $f(x_1) > 0$ and $f(x_2) < 0$, then we can be certain that there is at least one zero between $x_1$ and $x_2$ (provided that we know that $f$ is continuous). In this case we would say that $x_1$ and $x_2$ bracket a zero.

Here's what this scenario might look like on a graph:

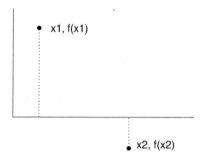

If this was all you knew about $f$, where would you go looking for a zero? If you said "halfway between $x_1$ and $x_2$," then congratulations! You just invented a numerical method called bisection!

If you said, "I would connect the dots with a straight line and compute the zero of the line," then congratulations! You just invented the secant method!

And if you said, "I would evaluate $f$ at a third point, find the parabola that passes through all three points, and compute the zeros of the parabola," then... well, you probably didn't say that.

Finally, if you said, "I would use a built-in MATLAB function that combines the best features of several efficient and robust numerical methods," then you are ready to go on to the next section.

## 6.6 `fzero`

`fzero` is a built-in MATLAB function that combines the best features of several efficient and robust numerical methods.

In order to use `fzero`, you have to define a MATLAB function that computes the error function you derived from the original nonlinear equation, and you have to provide an initial guess at the location of a zero.

We've already seen an example of an error function:

```
function res = error_func(x)
    res = x^2 - 2*x -3;
end
```

You can call `error_func` from the Command Window, and confirm that there are zeros at 3 and -1.

```
>> error_func(3)
ans = 0

>> error_func(-1)
ans = 0
```

But let's pretend that we don't know exactly where the roots are; we only know that one of them is near 4. Then we could call `fzero` like this:

```
>> fzero(@error_func, 4)
ans = 3.0000
```

Success! We found one of the zeros.

The first argument is a **function handle** that names the M-file that evaluates the error function. The @ symbol allows us to name the function without calling it. The interesting thing here is that you are not actually calling `error_func` directly; you are just telling `fzero` where it is. In turn, `fzero` calls your error function—more than once, in fact.

The second argument is the initial guess. If we provide a different initial guess, we get a different root (at least sometimes).

```
>> fzero(@error_func, -2)
ans = -1
```

Alternatively, if you know two values that bracket the root, you can provide both:

```
>> fzero(@error_func, [2,4])

ans = 3
```

The second argument here is actually a vector that contains two elements. The bracket operator is a convenient way (one of several) to create a new vector.

You might be curious to know how many times fzero calls your function, and where. If you modify error_func so that it displays the value of x every time it is called and then run fzero again, you get:

```
>> fzero(@error_func, [2,4])
x = 2
x = 4
x = 2.75000000000000
x = 3.03708133971292
x = 2.99755211623500
x = 2.99997750209270
x = 3.00000000025200
x = 3.00000000000000
x = 3
x = 3
ans = 3
```

Not surprisingly, it starts by computing $f(2)$ and $f(4)$. After each iteration, the interval that brackets the root gets smaller; fzero stops when the interval is so small that the estimated zero is correct to 16 digits. If you don't need that much precision, you can tell fzero to give you a quicker, dirtier answer (see the documentation for details).

## 6.7   What could go wrong?

The most common problem people have with fzero is leaving out the @. In that case, you get something like:

```
>> fzero(error_func, [2,4])
??? Input argument "x" is undefined.

Error in ==> error_func at 2
    x
```

Which is a very confusing error message. The problem is that MATLAB treats the first argument as a function call, so it calls error_func with no arguments. Since error_func requires one argument, the message indicates that the input argument is "undefined," although it might be clearer to say that you haven't provided a value for it.

Another common problem is writing an error function that never assigns a value to the output variable. In general, functions should *always* assign a value to the output variable, but MATLAB doesn't enforce this rule, so it is easy to forget. For example, if you write:

```
function res = error_func(x)
    y = x^2 - 2*x -3
end
```

and then call it from the Command Window:

```
>> error_func(4)
```

```
y = 5
```

It looks like it worked, but don't be fooled. This function assigns a value to y, and it displays the result, but when the function ends, y disappears along with the function's workspace. If you try to use it with fzero, you get

```
>> fzero(@error_func, [2,4])
```

```
y = -3
```

```
??? Error using ==> fzero
FZERO cannot continue because user supplied function_handle ==>
error_func failed with the error below.
```

```
Output argument "res" (and maybe others) not assigned during
call to "/home/downey/error_func.m (error_func)".
```

If you read it carefully, this is a pretty good error message (with the quibble that "output argument" is not a good synonym for "output variable").

You would have seen the same error message when you called error_func from the interpreter, if only you had assigned the result to a variable:

```
>> x = error_func(4)
```

```
y = 5
```

```
??? Output argument "res" (and maybe others) not assigned during
call to "/home/downey/error_func.m (error_func)".
```

```
Error in ==> error_func at 2
    y = x^2 - 2*x -3
```

You can avoid all of this if you remember these two rules:

- Functions should always assign values to their output variables[1].

- When you call a function, you should always do something with the result (either assign it to a variable or use it as part of an expression, etc.).

When you write your own functions and use them yourself, it is easy for mistakes to go undetected. But when you use your functions with MATLAB functions like fzero, you have to get it right!

Yet another thing that can go wrong: if you provide an interval for the initial guess and it doesn't actually contain a root, you get

---

[1]Well, ok, there are exceptions, including find_triples. Functions that don't return a value are sometimes called "commands," because they do something (like display values or generate a figure) but either don't have an output variable or don't make an assignment to it.

```
>> fzero(@error_func, [0,1])
```

```
??? Error using ==> fzero
The function values at the interval endpoints must differ in sign.
```

There is one other thing that can go wrong when you use `fzero`, but this one is less likely to be your fault. It is possible that `fzero` won't be able to find a root.

`fzero` is generally pretty robust, so you may never have a problem, but you should remember that there is no guarantee that `fzero` will work, especially if you provide a single value as an initial guess. Even if you provide an interval that brackets a root, things can still go wrong if the error function is discontinuous.

## 6.8   Finding an initial guess

The better your initial guess (or interval) is, the more likely it is that `fzero` will work, and the fewer iterations it will need.

When you are solving problems in the real world, you will usually have some intuition about the answer. This intuition is often enough to provide a good initial guess for zero-finding.

Another approach is to plot the function and see if you can approximate the zeros visually. If you have a function, like **error_func** that takes a scalar input variable and returns a scalar output variable, you can plot it with **ezplot**:

```
>> ezplot(@error_func, [-2,5])
```

The first argument is a function handle; the second is the interval you want to plot the function in.

By default `ezplot` calls your function 100 times (each time with a different value of `x`, of course). So you probably want to make your function silent before you plot it.

## 6.9   More name collisions

Functions and variables occupy the same "name-space," which means that whenever a name appears in an expression, MATLAB starts by looking for a variable with that name, and if there isn't one, it looks for a function.

As a result, if you have a variable with the same name as a function, the variable **shadows** the function. For example, if you assign a value to `sin`, and then try to use the `sin` function, you *might* get an error:

```
>> sin = 3;
>> x = 5;
>> sin(x)
??? Index exceeds matrix dimensions.
```

In this example, the problem is clear. Since the value of `sin` is a scalar, and a scalar is really a 1x1 matrix, MATLAB tries to access the 5th element of the matrix and finds that there isn't one. Of course, if there were more distance between the assignment and the "function call," this message would be pretty confusing.

But the only thing worse than getting an error message is *not* getting an error message. If the value of `sin` was a vector, or if the value of `x` was smaller, you would really be in trouble.

```
>> sin = 3;
>> sin(1)

ans = 3
```

Just to review, the sine of 1 is not 3!

The converse error can also happen if you try to access an undefined variable that also happens to be the name of a function. For example, if you have a function named `f`, and then try to increment a variable named `f` (and if you forget to initialize `f`), you get

```
>> f = f+1
??? Error:  "f" previously appeared to be used as a function or
command, conflicting with its use here as the name of a variable.
 A possible cause of this error is that you forgot to initialize the
 variable, or you have initialized it implicitly using load or eval.
```

At least, that's what you get if you are lucky. If this happens inside a function, MATLAB tries to call `f` as a function, and you get this

```
??? Input argument "x" is undefined.

Error in ==> f at 3
y = x^2 - a
```

There is no universal way to avoid these kind of collisions, but you can improve your chances by choosing variable names that don't shadow existing functions, and by choosing function names that you are unlikely to use as variables. That's why in Section 6.3 I called the error function `error_func` rather than `f`. I often give functions names that end in `func`, so that helps, too.

## 6.10   Debugging in four acts

When you are debugging a program, and especially if you are working on a hard bug, there are four things to try:

**reading:** Examine your code, read it back to yourself, and check that it means what you meant to say.

**running:** Experiment by making changes and running different versions. Often if you display the right thing at the right place in the program, the problem becomes obvious, but sometimes you have to spend some time to build scaffolding.

**ruminating:** Take some time to think! What kind of error is it: syntax, run-time, logical? What information can you get from the error messages, or from the output of the program? What kind of error could cause the problem you're seeing? What did you change last, before the problem appeared?

**retreating:** At some point, the best thing to do is back off, undoing recent changes, until you get back to a program that works, and that you understand. Then you can starting rebuilding.

Beginning programmers sometimes get stuck on one of these activities and forget the others. Each activity comes with its own failure mode.

For example, reading your code might help if the problem is a typographical error, but not if the problem is a conceptual misunderstanding. If you don't understand what your program does, you can read it 100 times and never see the error, because the error is in your head.

Running experiments can help, especially if you run small, simple tests. But if you run experiments without thinking or reading your code, you might fall into a pattern I call "random walk programming," which is the process of making random changes until the program does the right thing. Needless to say, random walk programming can take a long time.

The way out is to take more time to think. Debugging is like an experimental science. You should have at least one hypothesis about what the problem is. If there are two or more possibilities, try to think of a test that would eliminate one of them.

Taking a break sometimes helps with the thinking. So does talking. If you explain the problem to someone else (or even yourself), you will sometimes find the answer before you finish asking the question.

But even the best debugging techniques will fail if there are too many errors, or if the code you are trying to fix is too big and complicated. Sometimes the best option is to retreat, simplifying the program until you get to something that works, and then rebuild.

Beginning programmers are often reluctant to retreat, because they can't stand to delete a line of code (even if it's wrong). If it makes you feel better, copy your program into another file before you start stripping it down. Then you can paste the pieces back in a little bit at a time.

To summarize, here's the Ninth Theorem of debugging:

> Finding a hard bug requires reading, running, ruminating, and sometimes retreating. If you get stuck on one of these activities, try the others.

## 6.11   Glossary

**analytic solution:** A way of solving an equation by performing algebraic operations and deriving an explicit way to compute a value that is only known implicitly.

**numerical solution:** A way of solving an equation by finding a numerical value that satisfies the equation, often approximately.

**numerical method:** A method (or algorithm) for generating a numerical solution.

**map:** A correspondence between the elements of one set (the range) and the elements of another (the domain). You can think of sequences, vectors and functions as different kinds of maps.

**range:** The set of values a map maps from.

**domain:** The set of values a map maps to.

**discrete set:** A set, like the integers, whose elements are countable.

**continuous set:** A set, like the real numbers, whose elements are not countable. You can think of floating-point numbers as a continuous set.

**zero (of a function):** A value in the range of a function that maps to 0.

**function handle:** In MATLAB, a function handle is a way of referring to a function by name (and passing it as an argument) without calling it.

**shadow:** A kind of name collision in which a new definition causes an existing definition to become invisible. In MATLAB, variable names can shadow built-in functions (with hilarious results).

## 6.12   Exercises

**Exercise 6.1**    *1. Write a function called* cheby6 *that evaluates the 6th Chebyshev polynomial. It should take an input variable,* x, *and return*

$$32x^6 - 48x^4 + 18x^2 - 1 \tag{6.1}$$

*2. Use* ezplot *to display a graph of this function in the interval from 0 to 1. Estimate the location of any zeros in this range.*

*3. Use* fzero *to find as many different roots as you can. Does* fzero *always find the root that is closest to the initial guess?*

**Exercise 6.2**   *The density of a duck,* $\rho$, *is* $0.3g/cm^3$ *(0.3 times the density of water).*

*The volume of a sphere[2] with radius* r *is* $\frac{4}{3}\pi r^3$.

*If a sphere with radius r is submerged in water to a depth d, the volume of the sphere below the water line is*

$$volume = \frac{\pi}{3}(3rd^2 - d^3) \quad as \ long \ as \quad d < 2r$$

---

[2]This example is adapted from Gerald and Wheatley, *Applied Numerical Analysis*, Fourth Edition, Addison-Wesley, 1989.

*An object floats at the level where the weight of the displaced water equals the total weight of the object.*

*Assuming that a duck is a sphere with radius 10 cm, at what depth does a duck float?*

*Here are some suggestions about how to proceed:*

- *Write an equation relating $\rho$, $d$ and $r$.*

- *Rearrange the equation so the right-hand side is zero. The goal is to find values of $d$ that are roots of this equation.*

- *Write a MATLAB function that evaluates this function. Test it, then make it a quiet function.*

- *Make a guess about the value of $d_0$ to use as a starting place.*

- *Use `fzero` to find a root near $d_0$.*

- *Check to make sure the result makes sense. In particular, check that $d < 2r$, because otherwise the volume equation doesn't work!*

- *Try different values of $\rho$ and $r$ and see if you get the effect you expect. What happens as $\rho$ increases? Goes to infinity? Goes to zero? What happens as $r$ increases? Goes to infinity? Goes to zero?*

# Chapter 7

# Functions of vectors

## 7.1 Functions and files

So far we have only put one function in each file. It is also possible to put more than one function in a file, but only the first one, the **top-level function** can be called from the Command Window. The other **helper functions** can be called from anywhere inside the file, but not from any other file.

Large programs almost always require more than one function; keeping all the functions in one file is convenient, but it makes debugging difficult because you can't call helper functions from the Command Window.

To help with this problem, I often use the top-level function to develop and test my helper functions. For example, to write a program for Exercise 6.2, I would create a file named duck.m and start with a top-level function named duck that takes no input variables and returns no output value.

Then I would write a function named error_func to evaluate the error function for fzero. To test error_func I would call it from duck and then call duck from the Command Window.

Here's what my first draft might look like:

```
function res = duck()
    error = error_func(10)
end

function res = error_func(h)
    rho = 0.3;      % density in g / cm^3
    r = 10;         % radius in cm
    res = h;
end
```

The line res = h isn't finished yet, but this is enough code to test. Once I finished and tested error_func, I would modify duck to use fzero.

For this problem I might only need two functions, but if there were more, I could write and test them one at a time, and then combine them into a working program.

## 7.2 Physical modeling

Most of the examples so far have been about mathematics; Exercise 6.2, the "duck problem," is the first example we have seen of a physical system. If you didn't work on this exercise, you should at least go back and read it.

This book is supposed to be about **physical modeling**, so it might be a good idea to explain what that is. Physical modeling is a process for making predictions about physical systems and explaining their behavior. A **physical system** is something in the real world that we are interested in, like a duck.

The following figure shows the steps of this process:

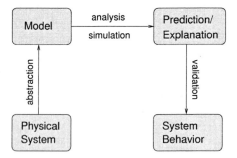

A **model** is a simplified description of a physical system. The process of building a model is called **abstraction**. In this context, "abstract" is the opposite of "realistic;" an abstract model bears little direct resemblance to the physical system it models, in the same way that abstract art does not directly depict objects in the real world. A realistic model is one that includes more details and corresponds more directly to the real world.

Abstraction involves making justified decisions about which factors to include in the model and which factors can be simplified or ignored. For example, in the duck problem, we took into account the density of the duck and the buoyancy of water, but we ignored the buoyancy of the duck due to displacement of air and the dynamic effect of paddling feet. We also simplified the geometry of the duck by assuming that the underwater parts of a duck are similar to a segment of a sphere. And we used coarse estimates of the size and weight of the duck.

Some of these decisions are justifiable. The density of the duck is much higher than the density of air, so the effect of buoyancy in air is probably small. Other decisions, like the spherical geometry, are harder to justify, but very helpful. The actual geometry of a duck is complicated; the sphere model makes it possible to generate an approximate answer without making detailed measurements of real ducks.

A more realistic model is not necessarily better. Models are useful because they can be analyzed mathematically and simulated computationally. Models that are too realistic might be difficult to simulate and impossible to analyze.

A model is successful if it is good enough for its purpose. If we only need a rough idea of the fraction of a duck that lies below the surface, the sphere model is good enough. If we need a more precise answer (for some reason) we might need a more realistic model.

Checking whether a model is good enough is called **validation**. The strongest form of validation is to make a measurement of an actual physical system and compare it to the prediction of a model.

If that is infeasible, there are weaker forms of validation. One is to compare multiple models of the same system. If they are inconsistent, that is an indication that (at least) one of them is wrong, and the size of the discrepancy is a hint about the reliability of their predictions.

We have only seen one physical model so far, so parts of this discussion may not be clear yet. We will come back to these topics later, but first we should learn more about vectors.

## 7.3 Vectors as input variables

Since many of the built-in functions take vectors as arguments, it should come as no surprise that you can write functions that take vectors. Here's a simple (silly) example:

```
function res = display_vector(X)
    X
end
```

There's nothing special about this function at all. The only difference from the scalar functions we've seen is that I used a capital letter to remind me that X is a vector.

This is another example of a function that doesn't actually have a return value; it just displays the value of the input variable:

```
>> display_vector(1:3)
```

```
X = 1    2    3
```

Here's a more interesting example that encapsulates the code from Section 4.12 that adds up the elements of a vector:

```
function res = mysum(X)
    total = 0;
    for i=1:length(X)
        total = total + X(i);
    end
    res = total;
end
```

I called it `mysum` to avoid a collision with the built-in function `sum`, which does pretty much the same thing.

Here's how you call it from the Command Window:

```
>> total = mysum(1:3)
```

```
total = 6
```

Because this function has a return value, I made a point of assigning it to a variable.

## 7.4   Vectors as output variables

There's also nothing wrong with assigning a vector to an output variable. Here's an example that encapsulates the code from Section 4.13:

```
function res = myapply(X)
    for i=1:length(X)
        Y(i) = X(i)^2
    end
    res = Y
end
```

Ideally I would have changed the name of the output variable to `Res`, as a reminder that it is supposed to get a vector value, but I didn't.

Here's how `myapply` works:

```
>> V = myapply(1:3)

V = 1     4     9
```

**Exercise 7.1**   *Write a function named* `find_target` *that encapsulates the code, from Section 4.14, that finds the location of a target value in a vector.*

## 7.5   Vectorizing your functions

Functions that work on vectors will almost always work on scalars as well, because MATLAB considers a scalar to be a vector with length 1.

```
>> mysum(17)

ans = 17

>> myapply(9)

ans = 81
```

Unfortunately, the converse is not always true. If you write a function with scalar inputs in mind, it might not work on vectors.

But it might! If the operators and functions you use in the body of your function work on vectors, then your function will probably work on vectors.

For example, here is the very first function we wrote:

```
function res = myfunc (x)
    s = sin(x)
    c = cos(x)
    res = abs(s) + abs(c)
end
```

And lo! It turns out to work on vectors:

```
>> Y = myfunc(1:3)

Y = 1.3818    1.3254    1.1311
```

At this point, I want to take a minute to acknowledge that I have been a little harsh in my presentation of MATLAB, because there are a number of features that I think make life harder than it needs to be for beginners. But here, finally, we are seeing features that show MATLAB's strengths.

Some of the other functions we wrote don't work on vectors, but they can be patched up with just a little effort. For example, here's `hypotenuse` from Section 5.5:

```
function res = hypotenuse(a, b)
    res = sqrt(a^2 + b^2);
end
```

This doesn't work on vectors because the `^` operator tries to do matrix exponentiation, which only works on square matrices.

```
>> hypotenuse(1:3, 1:3)
??? Error using ==> mpower
Matrix must be square.
```

But if you replace `^` with the elementwise operator `.^`, it works!

```
>> A = [3,5,8];
>> B = [4,12,15];
>> C = hypotenuse(A, B)

C = 5    13    17
```

In this case, it matches up corresponding elements from the two input vectors, so the elements of C are the hypotenuses of the pairs $(3, 4)$, $(5, 12)$ and $(8, 15)$, respectively.

In general, if you write a function using only elementwise operators and functions that work on vectors, then the new function will also work on vectors.

# 7.6   Sums and differences

Another common vector operation is **cumulative sum**, which takes a vector as an input and computes a new vector that contains all of the partial sums of the original. In math notation, if $V$ is the original vector, then the elements of the cumulative sum, $C$, are:

$$C_i = \sum_{j=1}^{i} V_j$$

In other words, the $i$th element of $C$ is the sum of the first $i$ elements from $V$. MATLAB provides a function named `cumsum` that computes cumulative sums:

```
>> V = 1:5

V = 1     2     3     4     5

>> C = cumsum(V)

C = 1     3     6     10     15
```

**Exercise 7.2**  *Write a function named* `cumulative_sum` *that uses a loop to compute the cumulative sum of the input vector.*

The inverse operation of `cumsum` is `diff`, which computes the difference between successive elements of the input vector.

```
>> D = diff(C)

D = 2     3     4     5
```

Notice that the output vector is shorter by one than the input vector. As a result, MATLAB's version of `diff` is not exactly the inverse of `cumsum`. If it were, then we would expect `cumsum(diff(X))` to be X:

```
>> cumsum(diff(V))

ans = 1     2     3     4
```

But it isn't.

**Exercise 7.3**  *Write a function named* `mydiff` *that computes the inverse of* `cumsum`, *so that* `cumsum(mydiff(X))` *and* `mydiff(cumsum(X))` *both return X.*

## 7.7   Products and ratios

The multiplicative version of `cumsum` is `cumprod`, which computes the **cumulative product**. In math notation, that's:

$$P_i = \prod_{j=1}^{i} V_j$$

In MATLAB, that looks like:

```
>> V = 1:5

V = 1     2     3     4     5

>> P = cumprod(V)

P = 1     2     6     24     120
```

**Exercise 7.4** *Write a function named* `cumulative_prod` *that uses a loop to compute the cumulative product of the input vector.*

MATLAB doesn't provide the multiplicative version of `diff`, which would be called `ratio`, and which would compute the ratio of successive elements of the input vector.

**Exercise 7.5** *Write a function named* `myratio` *that computes the inverse of* `cumprod`, *so that* `cumprod(myratio(X))` *and* `myratio(cumprod(X))` *both return* `X`.

*You can use a loop, or if you want to be clever, you can take advantage of the fact that $e^{\ln a + \ln b} = ab$.*

*If you apply* `myratio` *to a vector that contains Fibonacci numbers, you can confirm that the ratio of successive elements converges on the golden ratio, $(1 + \sqrt{5})/2$ (see Exercise 4.6).*

## 7.8   Existential quantification

It is often useful to check the elements of a vector to see if there are any that satisfy a condition. For example, you might want to know if there are any positive elements. In logic, this condition is called **existential quantification**, and it is denoted with the symbol $\exists$, which is pronounced "there exists." For example, this expression

$$\exists x \text{ in } S : x > 0$$

means, "there exists some element $x$ in the set $S$ such that $x > 0$." In MATLAB it is natural to express this idea with a logical function, like `exists`, that returns 1 if there is such an element and 0 if there is not.

```
function res = exists(X)
    for i=1:length(X)
        if X(i) > 0
            res = 1;
            return
        end
    end
    res = 0;
end
```

We haven't seen the **return** statement before; it is similar to **break** except that it breaks out of the whole function, not just the loop. That behavior is what we want here because as soon as we find a positive element, we know the answer (it exists!) and we can end the function immediately without looking at the rest of the elements.

If we exit at the end of the loop, that means we didn't find what we were looking for (because if we had, we would have hit the **return** statement).

## 7.9   Universal quantification

Another common operation on vectors is to check whether *all* of the elements satisfy a condition, which is known to logicians as **universal quantification** and denoted with the symbol ∀ which is pronounced "for all." So this expression

$$\forall x \text{ in } S : x > 0$$

means "for all elements, $x$, in the set $S$, $x > 0$."

A slightly silly way to evaluate this expression in MATLAB is to count the number of elements that satisfy the condition. A better way is to reduce the problem to existential quantification; that is, to rewrite

$$\forall x \text{ in } S : x > 0$$

as

$$\sim \exists x \text{ in } S : x \leq 0$$

Where $\sim \exists$ means "does not exist." In other words, checking that all the elements are positive is the same as checking that there are no elements that are non-positive.

**Exercise 7.6**   *Write a function named* `forall` *that takes a vector and returns 1 if all of the elements are positive and 0 if there are any non-positive elements.*

## 7.10   Logical vectors

When you apply a logical operator to a vector, the result is a **logical vector**; that is, a vector whose elements are the logical values 1 and 0.

```
>> V = -3:3

V = -3    -2    -1    0    1    2    3

>> L = V>0

L =  0    0    0    0    1    1    1
```

In this example, L is a logical vector whose elements correspond to the elements of V. For each positive element of V, the corresponding element of L is 1.

Logical vectors can be used like flags to store the state of a condition. They are also often used with the `find` function, which takes a logical vector and returns a vector that contains the indices of the elements that are "true."

Applying `find` to L yields

```
>> find(L)
```

```
ans = 5    6    7
```

which indicates that elements 5, 6 and 7 have the value 1.

If there are no "true" elements, the result is an empty vector.

```
>> find(V>10)
```

```
ans = Empty matrix: 1-by-0
```

This example computes the logical vector and passes it as an argument to `find` without assigning it to an intermediate variable. You can read this version abstractly as "find the indices of elements of V that are greater than 10."

We can also use `find` to write `exists` more concisely:

```
function res = exists(X)
    L = find(X>0)
    res = length(L) > 0
end
```

**Exercise 7.7** *Write a version of* `forall` *using* `find`.

## 7.11  Glossary

**top-level function:** The first function in an M-file; it is the only function that can be called from the Command Window or from another file.

**helper function:** A function in an M-file that is not the top-level function; it only be called from another function in the same file.

**physical modeling:** A process for making predictions about physical systems and explaining their behavior.

**physical system:** Something in the real world that we are interested in studying.

**model :** A simplified description of a physical system that lends itself to analysis or simulation.

**abstraction:** The process of building a model by making decisions about what factors to simplify or ignore.

**validation:** Checking whether a model is adequate for its purpose.

**existential quantification:** A logical condition that expresses the idea that "there exists" an element of a set with a certain property.

**universal quantification:** A logical condition that expresses the idea that all elements of a set have a certain property.

**logical vector:** A vector, usually the result of applying a logical operator to a vector, that contains logical values 1 and 0.

# Chapter 8

# Ordinary Differential Equations

## 8.1 Differential equations

A **differential equation** (DE) is an equation that describes the derivatives of an unknown function. "Solving a DE" means finding a function whose derivatives satisfy the equation.

For example, when bacteria grow in particularly bacteria-friendly conditions, the rate of growth at any point in time is proportional to the current population. What we might like to know is the population as a function of time. Toward that end, let's define $f$ to be a function that maps from time, $t$, to population $y$. We don't know what it is, but we can write a differential equation that describes it:

$$\frac{df}{dt} = af$$

where $a$ is a constant that characterizes how quickly the population increases.

Notice that both sides of the equation are functions. To say that two functions are equal is to say that their values are equal at all times. In other words:

$$\forall t : \frac{df}{dt}(t) = af(t)$$

This is an **ordinary** differential equation (ODE) because all the derivatives involved are taken with respect to the same variable. If the equation related derivatives with respect to different variables (partial derivatives), it would be a **partial** differential equation.

This equation is **first order** because it involves only first derivatives. If it involved second derivatives, it would be second order, and so on.

This equation is **linear** because each term involves $t$, $f$ or $df/dt$ raised to the first power; if any of the terms involved products or powers of $t$, $f$ and $df/dt$ it would be nonlinear.

Linear, first order ODEs can be solved analytically; that is, we can express the solution as a function of $t$. This particular ODE has an infinite number of solutions, but they all have this form:

$$t \rightarrow be^{at}$$

For any value of $b$, this function satisfies the ODE. If you don't believe me, take its derivative and check.

If we know the population of bacteria at a particular point in time, we can use that additional information to determine which of the infinite solutions is the (unique) one that describes a particular population over time.

For example, if we know that $f(0) = 5$ billion cells, then we can write

$$f(0) = 5 = be^{a0}$$

and solve for $b$, which is 5. That determines what we wanted to know:

$$f : t \rightarrow 5e^{at}$$

The extra bit of information that determines $b$ is called the **initial condition** (although it isn't always specified at $t = 0$).

Unfortunately, most interesting physical systems are described by nonlinear DEs, most of which can't be solved analytically. The alternative is to solve them numerically.

## 8.2    Euler's method

The simplest numerical method for ODEs is Euler's method. Here's a test to see if you are as smart as Euler. Let's say that you arrive at time $t$ and measure the current population, $y$, and the rate of change, $r$. What do you think the population will be after some period of time $h$ has elapsed?

If you said $y + rh$, congratulations! You just invented Euler's method (but you're still not as smart as Euler).

This estimate is based on the assumption that $r$ is constant, but in general it's not, so we only expect the estimate to be good if $r$ changes slowly and $h$ is small.

But let's assume (for now) that the ODE we are interested in can be written so that

$$\forall t, y : \frac{df}{dt}(t) = g(t, y)$$

where $y = f(t)$ and $g$ is some function that maps $(t, y)$ onto $r$; that is, given the time and current population, it computes the rate of change. Then we can advance from one point in time to the next using these equations:

$$T_{n+1} = T_n + h \tag{8.1}$$
$$F_{n+1} = F_n + g(t, y)h \tag{8.2}$$

where $T$ is a sequence of times where we estimate the value of $f$, and $F$ is the sequence of estimates. For each index $i$, $F_i$ is an estimate of $f(T_i)$. The interval $h$ is called the **time step**.

Assuming that we start at $t = 0$ and we have an initial condition $f(0) = y_0$ (where $y_0$ denotes a particular, known value), we would set $T_1 = 0$ and $F_1 = y_0$, and then use Equations 8.1 and 8.2 to compute values of $T_i$ and $F_i$ until $T_i$ gets to the value of $t$ we are interested in.

If the rate doesn't change too fast and the time step isn't too big, Euler's method is accurate enough for most purposes. One way to check is to run it once with time step $h$ and then run it again with time step $h/2$. If the results are the same, they are probably accurate; otherwise, cut the time step again.

Euler's method is **first order**, which means that each time you cut the time step in half, you expect the estimation error to drop by half. With a second-order method, you expect the error to drop by a factor of 4; third-order drops by 8, etc. The price of higher order methods is that they have to evaluate $g$ more times per time step.

## 8.3   Another note on notation

There's a lot of math notation in this chapter, and some of it is non-standard, so I want to pause to review what we have so far. Here are the variables, their meanings, and their types:

| Name | Meaning | Type |
|------|---------|------|
| $f$ | The unknown function specified, implicitly, by an ODE. | function $t \to y$ |
| $df/dt$ | The first time derivative of $f$ | function $t \to r$ |
| $f_t$ | Alternative notation for the first time derivative of $f$ | function $t \to r$ |
| $g$ | A "rate function," derived from the ODE, that computes rate of change for any $t, y$. | function $t, y \to r$ |
| $t$ | time | scalar variable |
| $y$ | population | scalar variable |
| $r$ | rate of change | scalar variable |
| $h$ | time step | scalar constant |
| $T$ | a sequence of times, $t$, where we estimate $f(t)$ | sequence |
| $F$ | a sequence of estimates for $f(t)$ | sequence |

So $f$ is a function that computes the population as a function of time, $f(t)$ is the function evaluated at a particular time, and if we assign $f(t)$ to a variable, we usually call that variable $y$. Similarly, $g$ is a "rate function" that computes the rate of change as a function of time and population. If we assign $g(t,y)$ to a variable, we call it $r$.

$df/dt$ is the most common notation for the first derivative of $f$, but I have never liked it because it looks like a fraction. I prefer $f_t$, which has the benefit of looking like a function.

It is easy to get $f_t$ confused with $g$, but notice that they are not even the same type. $g$ is more general: it can compute the rate of change for any (hypothetical) population at any time; $f_t$ is more specific: it is the actual rate of change at time $t$, given that the population is $f(t)$.

## 8.4   ode45

A limitation of Euler's method is that the time step is constant from one iteration to the next. But some parts of the solution are harder to estimate than others; if the time step is small enough to get the hard parts right, it is doing more work than necessary on the easy parts. The ideal solution is to adjust the time step as you go along. Methods that do that are called **adaptive**, and one of the best adaptive methods is the Dormand-Prince pair of Runge-Kutta formulas. Fortunately, you don't have to know what that means, because the nice people at Mathworks have implemented it in a function called **ode45**. The **ode** stands for "ordinary differential equation [solver];" the 45 indicates that it uses a combination of 4th and 5th order formulas.

In order to use **ode45**, you have to write a MATLAB function that evaluates $g$ as a function of $t$ and $y$.

As an example, suppose that the rate of population growth for rats depends on the current population, $y$, and the availability of food, which varies over the course of the year. The governing equation might be something like

$$f_t = af \left[1 + \sin(\omega t)\right]$$

where $a$ is a **parameter**[1] that characterizes the reproductive rate, and $\omega$ is the frequency of a periodic function that characterizes the effect of varying food supply on reproduction.

This is an equation that specifies a relationship between a function and its derivative. In order to estimate values of $f$ numerically, we have to transform it into a rate function. The first step is to write the equation more explicitly; to say that two function are equal means that they are equal all all times. In other words

$$\forall t : f_t(t) = af(t)\left[1 + \sin(\omega t)\right]$$

---

[1] A parameter is a value that appears in a model to quantify some physical aspect of the scenario being modeled. For example, in Exercise 6.2 we used parameters rho and r to quantify the density and radius of a duck. Parameters are often constants, but in some models they might vary in time.

where $t$ is time in days. The next step is to introduce a variable, $y$, as another name for $f(t)$

$$\forall t : f_t(t) = ay\left[1 + \sin(\omega t)\right]$$

This equation means that if we are given $t$ and $y$, we can compute $f_t(t)$, which is the slope, or rate of change, of $f$. The last step is to express that computation as a function called $g$:

$$g : t, y \rightarrow ay\left[1 + \sin(\omega t)\right]$$

This function is useful because we can use it with Euler's method or **ode45** to estimate values of $f$. All we have to do is write a function that evaluates $g$. Here's what that looks like using the values $a = 0.01$ and $\omega = 2\pi/365$ (one cycle per year):

```
function res = rats(t, y)
    a = 0.01;
    omega = 2 * pi / 365;
    res = a * y * (1 + sin(omega * t));
end
```

You can test this function from the Command Window by calling it with different values of t and y; the result is the rate of change (in units of rats per day):

```
>> r = rats(0, 2)
```

```
r = 0.0200
```

So if there are two rats on January 1, we expect them to reproduce at a rate that would produce 2 more rats per hundred days. But if we come back in April, the rate has almost doubled:

```
>> r = rats(120, 2)
```

```
r = 0.0376
```

Since the rate is constantly changing, it is not easy to predict the future rat population, but that is exactly what **ode45** does. Here's how you would use it:

```
>> ode45(@rats, [0, 365], 2)
```

The first argument is a handle for the function that computes $g$. The second argument is the interval we are interested in, one year. The third argument is the initial population, $f(0) = 2$.

When you call **ode45** without assigning the result to a variable, MATLAB displays the result in a figure:

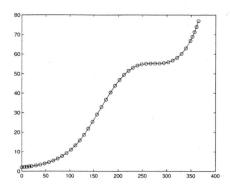

The x-axis shows time from 0 to 365 days; the y-axis shows the rat population, which starts at 2 and grows to almost 80. The rate of growth is slow in the winter and summer, and faster in the spring and fall, but it also accelerates as the population grows.

## 8.5   Multiple output variables

ode45 is one of many MATLAB functions that return more than one output variable. The syntax for calling it and saving the results is

```
>> [T, Y] = ode45(@rats, [0, 365], 2);
```

The first return value is assigned to T; the second is assigned to Y. Each element of T is a time, $t$, where ode45 estimated the population; each element of Y is an estimate of $f(t)$.

If you assign the output values to variables, ode45 doesn't draw the figure; you have to do it yourself:

```
>> plot(T, Y, 'bo-')
```

If you plot the elements of T, you'll see that the space between the points is not quite even. They are closer together at the beginning of the interval and farther apart at the end.

To see the population at the end of the year, you can display the last element from each vector:

```
>> [T(end), Y(end)]
```

```
ans = 365.0000    76.9530
```

end is a special word in MATLAB; when it appears as an index, it means "the index of the last element." You can use it in an expression, so Y(end-1) is the second-to-last element of Y.

How much does the final population change if you double the initial population? How much does it change if you double the interval to two years? How much does it change if you double the value of $a$?

## 8.6 Analytic or numerical?

When you solve an ODE analytically, the result is a function, $f$, that allows you to compute the population, $f(t)$, for any value of $t$. When you solve an ODE numerically, you get two vectors. You can think of these vectors as a discrete approximation of the continuous function $f$: "discrete" because it is only defined for certain values of $t$, and "approximate" because each value $F_i$ is only an estimate of the true value $f(t)$.

So those are the limitations of numerical solutions. The primary advantage is that you can compute numerical solutions to ODEs that don't have analytic solutions, which is the vast majority of nonlinear ODEs.

If you are curious to know more about how ode45 works, you can modify rats to display the points, $(t, y)$, where ode45 evaluates $g$. Here is a simple version:

```
function res = rats(t, y)
    plot(t, y, 'bo')
    a = 0.01;
    omega = 2 * pi / 365;
    res = a * y * (1 + sin(omega * t));
end
```

Each time rats is called, it plots one data point; in order to see all of the data points, you have to use hold on.

```
>> clf; hold on
>> [T, Y] = ode45(@rats, [0, 10], 2);
```

This figure shows part of the output, zoomed in on the range from Day 100 to 170:

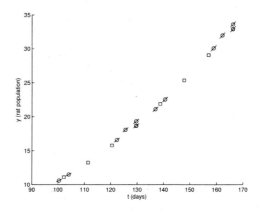

The circles show the points where ode45 called rats. The lines through the circles show the slope (rate of change) calculated at each point. The rectangles show the locations of the estimates $(T_i, F_i)$. Notice that ode45 typically evaluates $g$ several times for each estimate. This allows it to improve the estimates, for one thing, but also to detect places where the errors are increasing so it can decrease the time step (or the other way around).

## 8.7   What can go wrong?

Don't forget the @ on the function handle. If you leave it out, MATLAB treats the first argument as a function call, and calls rats without providing arguments.

```
>> ode45(rats, [0,365], 2)
??? Input argument "y" is undefined.

Error in ==> rats at 4
    res = a * y * (1 + sin(omega * t));
```

Again, the error message is confusing, because it looks like the problem is in rats. You've been warned!

Also, remember that the function you write will be called by ode45, which means it has to have the signature ode45 expects: it should take two input variables, t and y, in that order, and return one output variable, r.

If you are working with a rate function like this:

$$g : t, y \rightarrow ay$$

You might be tempted to write this:

```
function res = rate_func(y)          % WRONG
    a = 0.1
    res = a * y
end
```

But that would be wrong. So very wrong. Why? Because when ode45 calls rate_func, it provides two arguments. If you only take one input variable, you'll get an error. So you have to write a function that takes t as an input variable, even if you don't use it.

```
function res = rate_func(t, y)       % RIGHT
    a = 0.1
    res = a * y
end
```

Another common error is to write a function that doesn't make an assignment to the output variable. If you write something like this:

```
function res = rats(t, y)
    a = 0.01;
    omega = 2 * pi / 365;
    r = a * y * (1 + sin(omega * t))    % WRONG
end
```

And then call it from ode45, you get

```
>> ode45(@rats, [0,365], 2)
??? Output argument "res" (and maybe others) not assigned during
call to "/home/downey/rats.m (rats)".
```

```
Error in ==> rats at 2
   a = 0.01;

Error in ==> funfun/private/odearguments at 110
f0 = feval(ode,t0,y0,args{:});   % ODE15I sets args{1} to yp0.

Error in ==> ode45 at 173
[neq, tspan, ntspan, next, t0, tfinal, tdir, y0, f0, odeArgs,
odeFcn, ...
```

This might be a scary message, but if you read the first line and ignore the rest, you'll get the idea.

Yet another mistake that people make with **ode45** is leaving out the brackets on the second argument. In that case, MATLAB thinks there are four arguments, and you get

```
>> ode45(@rats, 0, 365, 2)
??? Error using ==> funfun/private/odearguments
When the first argument to ode45 is a function handle, the
tspan argument must have at least two elements.

Error in ==> ode45 at 173
[neq, tspan, ntspan, next, t0, tfinal, tdir, y0, f0, odeArgs,
odeFcn, ...
```

Again, if you read the first line, you should be able to figure out the problem (**tspan** stands for "time span", which we have been calling the interval).

## 8.8 Stiffness

There is yet another problem you might encounter, but if it makes you feel better, it might not be your fault: the problem you are trying to solve might be **stiff**[2].

I won't give a technical explanation of stiffness here, except to say that for some problems (over some intervals with some initial conditions) the time step needed to control the error is very small, which means that the computation takes a long time. Here's one example:

$$f_t = f^2 - f^3$$

If you solve this ODE with the initial condition $f(0) = \delta$ over the interval from 0 to $2/\delta$, with $\delta = 0.01$, you should see something like this:

---

[2]The following discussion is based partly on an article from Mathworks available at http://www.mathworks.com/company/newsletters/news_notes/clevescorner/may03_cleve.html

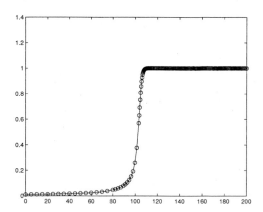

After the transition from 0 to 1, the time step is very small and the computation goes slowly. For smaller values of $\delta$, the situation is even worse.

In this case, the problem is easy to fix: instead of ode45 you can use ode23s, an ODE solver that tends to perform well on stiff problems (that's what the "s" stands for).

In general, if you find that ode45 is taking a long time, you might want to try one of the stiff solvers. It won't always solve the problem, but if the problem is stiffness, the improvement can be striking.

**Exercise 8.1** *Write a rate function for this ODE and use* ode45 *to solve it with the given initial condition and interval. Start with* $\delta = 0.1$ *and decrease it by multiples of 10. If you get tired of waiting for a computation to complete, you can press the Stop button in the Figure window or press Control-C in the Command Window.*

*Now replace* ode45 *with* ode23s *and try again!*

# 8.9   Glossary

**differential equation (DE):** An equation that relates the derivatives of an unknown function.

**ordinary DE:** A DE in which all derivatives are taken with respect to the same variable.

**partial DE:** A DE that includes derivatives with respect to more than one variable

**first order (ODE):** A DE that includes only first derivatives.

**linear:** A DE that includes no products or powers of the function and its derivatives.

**time step:** The interval in time between successive estimates in the numerical solution of a DE.

**first order (numerical method):** A method whose error is expected to halve when the time step is halved.

**adaptive:** A method that adjusts the time step to control error.

**stiffness:** A characteristic of some ODEs that makes some ODE solvers run slowly (or generate bad estimates). Some ODE solvers, like ode23s, are designed to work on stiff problems.

**parameter:** A value that appears in a model to quantify some physical aspect of the scenario being modeled.

## 8.10 Exercises

**Exercise 8.2** *Suppose that you are given an 8 ounce cup of coffee at 90 °C and a 1 ounce container of cream at room temperature, which is 20 °C. You have learned from bitter experience that the hottest coffee you can drink comfortably is 60 °C.*

*Assuming that you take cream in your coffee, and that you would like to start drinking as soon as possible, are you better off adding the cream immediately or waiting? And if you should wait, then how long?*

*To answer this question, you will have to model the cooling process of a hot liquid in air. Hot coffee transfers heat to the environment by conduction, radiation, and evaporative cooling. Quantifying these effects individually would be challenging and unnecessary to answer the question as posed.*

*As a simplification, we can use Newton's Law of Cooling[3]:*

$$f_t = -r(f - e)$$

*where f is the temperature of the coffee as a function of time and $f_t$ is its time derivative; e is the temperature of the environment, which is a constant in this case, and r is a parameter (also constant) that characterizes the rate of heat transfer.*

*It would be easy to estimate r for a given coffee cup by making a few measurements over time. Let's assume that that has been done and r has been found to be 0.001 in units of inverse seconds, 1/s.*

- *Using mathematical notation, write the rate function, g, as a function of y, where y is the temperature of the coffee at a particular point in time.*

- *Create an M-file named coffee and write a function called coffee that takes no input variables and returns no output value. Put a simple statement like x=5 in the body of the function and invoke coffee() from the Command Window.*

- *Add a function called rate_func that takes t and y and computes $g(t, y)$. Notice that in this case g does not actually depend on t; nevertheless, your function has to take t as the first input argument in order to work with ode45.*

  *Test your function by adding a line like rate_func(0,90) to coffee, the call coffee from the Command Window.*

[3]http://en.wikipedia.org/wiki/Heat_conduction

- *Once you get* `rate_func(0,90)` *working, modify* `coffee` *to use* `ode45` *to compute the temperature of the coffee (ignoring the cream) for 60 minutes. Confirm that the coffee cools quickly at first, then more slowly, and reaches room temperature (approximately) after about an hour.*

- *Write a function called* `mix_func` *that computes the final temperature of a mixture of two liquids. It should take the volumes and temperatures of the liquids as parameters.*

  *In general, the final temperature of a mixture depends on the specific heat of the two substances[4]. But if we make the simplifying assumption that coffee and cream have the same density and specific heat, then the final temperature is $(v_1y_1 + v_2y_2)/(v_1 + v_2)$, where $v_1$ and $v_2$ are the volumes of the liquids, and $y_1$ and $y_2$ are their temperatures.*

  *Add code to* `coffee` *to test* `mix_func`.

- *Use* `mix_func` *and* `ode45` *to compute the time until the coffee is drinkable if you add the cream immediately.*

- *Modify* `coffee` *so it takes an input variable t that determines how many seconds the coffee is allowed to cool before adding the cream, and returns the temperature of the coffee after mixing.*

- *Use* `fzero` *to find the time t that causes the temperature of the coffee after mixing to be 60 °C.*

- *What do these results tell you about the answer to the original question? Is the answer what you expected? What simplifying assumptions does this answer depend on? Which of them do you think has the biggest effect? Do you think it is big enough to affect the outcome? Overall, how confident are you that this model can give a definitive answer to this question? What might you do to improve it?*

---

[4]http://en.wikipedia.org/wiki/Heat_capacity

# Chapter 9

# Systems of ODEs

## 9.1 Matrices

A matrix is a two-dimensional version of a vector. Like a vector, it contains elements that are identified by indices. The difference is that the elements are arranged in rows and columns, so it takes *two* indices to identify an element.

One of many ways to create a matrix is the **magic** function, which returns a "magic" matrix with the given size:

```
>> M = magic(3)
```

```
M =   8    1    6
      3    5    7
      4    9    2
```

If you don't know the size of a matrix, you can use **whos** to display it:

```
>> whos
  Name        Size              Bytes  Class
  M           3x3                  72  double array
```

Or the **size** function, which returns a vector:

```
>> V = size(M)
```

```
V = 3     3
```

The first element is the number of rows, the second is the number of columns.

To read an element of a matrix, you specify the row and column numbers:

```
>> M(1,2)
```

```
ans = 1
```

```
>> M(2,1)
```

ans = 3

When you are working with matrices, it takes some effort to remember which index comes first, row or column. I find it useful to repeat "row, column" to myself, like a mantra. You might also find it helpful to remember "down, across," or the abbreviation RC.

Another way to create a matrix is to enclose the elements in brackets, with semi-colons between rows:

```
>> D = [1,2,3 ; 4,5,6]

D =   1     2     3
      4     5     6

>> size(D)

ans = 2     3
```

## 9.2   Row and column vectors

Although it is useful to think in terms of scalars, vectors and matrices, from MATLAB's point of view, everything is a matrix. A scalar is just a matrix that happens to have one row and one column:

```
>> x = 5;
>> size(x)

ans = 1     1
```

And a vector is a matrix with only one row:

```
>> R = 1:5;
>> size(R)

ans = 1     5
```

Well, some vectors, anyway. Actually, there are two kind of vectors. The ones we have seen so far are called **row vectors**, because the elements are arranged in a row; the other kind are **column vectors**, where the elements are in a single column.

One way to create a column vector is to create a matrix with only one element per row:

```
>> C = [1;2;3]

C =

    1
    2
    3
```

```
>> size(C)

ans = 3     1
```

The difference between row and column vectors is important in linear algebra, but for most basic vector operations, it doesn't matter. When you index the elements of a vector, you don't have to know what kind it is:

```
>> R(2)

ans = 2

>> C(2)

ans = 2
```

## 9.3    The transpose operator

The transpose operator, which looks remarkably like an apostrophe, computes the **transpose** of a matrix, which is a new matrix that has all of the elements of the original, but with each row transformed into a column (or you can think of it the other way around).

In this example:

```
>> D = [1,2,3 ; 4,5,6]

D =  1     2     3
     4     5     6
```

D has two rows, so its transpose has two columns:

```
>> Dt = D'

Dt = 1     4
     2     5
     3     6
```

**Exercise 9.1**   *What effect does the transpose operator have on row vectors, column vectors, and scalars?*

## 9.4    Lotka-Voltera

The Lotka-Voltera model describes the interactions between two species in an ecosystem, a predator and its prey. A common example is rabbits and foxes.

The model is governed by the following system of differential equations:

$$R_t = aR - bRF$$
$$F_t = ebRF - cF$$

where

- $R$ is the population of rabbits,
- $F$ is the population of foxes,
- $a$ is the natural growth rate of rabbits in the absence of predation,
- $c$ is the natural death rate of foxes in the absence of prey,
- $b$ is the death rate of rabbits per interaction with a fox,
- $e$ is the efficiency of turning eaten rabbits into foxes.

At first glance you might think you could solve these equations by calling ode45 once to solve for $R$ as a function of time and once to solve for $F$. The problem is that each equation involves both variables, which is what makes this a **system of equations** and not just a list of unrelated equations. To solve a system, you have to solve the equations simultaneously.

Fortunately, ode45 can handle systems of equations. The difference is that the initial condition is a vector that contains initial values $R(0)$ and $F(0)$, and the output is a matrix that contains one column for $R$ and one for $F$.

And here's what the rate function looks like with the parameters $a = 0.1$, $b = 0.01$, $c = 0.1$ and $e = 0.2$:

```
function res = lotka(t, V)
    % unpack the elements of V
    r = V(1);
    f = V(2);

    % set the parameters
    a = 0.1;
    b = 0.01;
    c = 0.1;
    e = 0.2;

    % compute the derivatives
    drdt = a*r - b*r*f;
    dfdt = e*b*r*f - c*f;

    % pack the derivatives into a vector
    res = [drdt; dfdt];
end
```

As usual, the first input variable is time. The second input variable is a vector with two elements, $R(t)$ and $F(t)$. I gave it a capital letter to remind me that it is a vector. The body of the function includes four **paragraphs**, each explained by a comment.

The first paragraph **unpacks** the vector by copying the elements into scalar variables. This isn't necessary, but giving names to these values helps me remember what's what. It also makes the third paragraph, where we compute the derivatives, resemble the mathematical equations we were given, which helps prevent errors.

The second paragraph sets the parameters that describe the reproductive rates of rabbits and foxes, and the characteristics of their interactions. If we were studying a real system, these values would come from observations of real animals, but for this example I chose values that yield interesting results.

The last paragraph **packs** the computed derivatives back into a vector. When `ode45` calls this function, it provides a vector as input and expects to get a vector as output.

Sharp-eyed readers will notice something different about this line:

```
res = [drdt; dfdt];
```

The semi-colon between the elements of the vector is not an error. It is necessary in this case because `ode45` requires the result of this function to be a column vector.

Now we can run `ode45` like this:

```
ode45(@lotka, [0, 365], [100, 10])
```

As always, the first argument is a function handle, the second is the time interval, and the third is the initial condition. The initial condition is a vector: the first element is the number of rabbits at $t = 0$, the second element is the number of foxes.

The order of these elements (rabbits and foxes) is up to you, but you have to be consistent. That is, the initial conditions you provide when you call `ode45` have to be the same as the order, inside `lotka`, where you unpack the input vector and repack the output vector. MATLAB doesn't know what these values mean; it is up to you as the programmer to keep track.

But if you get the order right, you should see something like this:

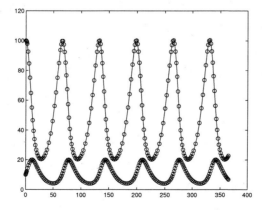

The x-axis is time in days; the y-axis is population. The top curve shows the population of rabbits; the bottom curve shows foxes. This result is one of several patterns this system can fall into, depending on the starting conditions and the parameters. As an exercise, try experimenting with different values.

## 9.5   What can go wrong?

The output vector from the rate function has to be a column vector; otherwise you get

```
??? Error using ==> funfun/private/odearguments
LOTKA must return a column vector.
```

```
Error in ==> ode45 at 173
[neq, tspan, ntspan, next, t0, tfinal, tdir, y0, f0, odeArgs,
odeFcn, ...
```

Which is pretty good as error messages go. It's not clear *why* it needs to be a column vector, but that's not our problem.

Another possible error is reversing the order of the elements in the initial conditions, or the vectors inside `lotka`. Again, MATLAB doesn't know what the elements are supposed to mean, so it can't catch errors like this; it will just produce incorrect results.

## 9.6   Output matrices

As we saw before, if you call `ode45` without assigning the results to variables, it plots the results. If you assign the results to variables, it suppresses the figure. Here's what that looks like:

```
>> [T, M] = ode45(@lotka, [0, 365], [100, 10]);
```

You can think of the left side of this assignment as a vector of variables.

As in previous examples, `T` is a vector of time values where `ode45` made estimates. But unlike previous examples, the second output variable is a matrix containing one column for each variable (in this case, $R$ and $F$) and one row for each time value.

```
>> size(M)
```

```
ans = 185     2
```

This structure—one column per variable—is a common way to use matrices. `plot` understands this structure, so if you do this:

```
>> plot(T, M)
```

MATLAB understands that it should plot each column from `M` versus `T`.

You can copy the columns of `M` into other variables like this:

```
>> R = M(:, 1);
>> F = M(:, 2);
```

In this context, the colon represents the range from 1 to `end`, so `M(:, 1)` means "all the rows, column 1" and `M(:, 2)` means "all the rows, column 2."

```
>> size(R)
```

```
ans = 185     1
```

```
>> size(F)
```

```
ans = 185      1
```

So R and F are column vectors.

If you plot these vectors against each other, like this

```
>> plot(R, F)
```

You get a **phase plot** that looks like this:

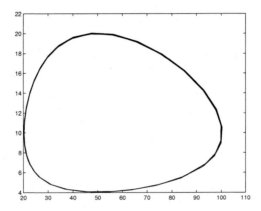

Each point on this plot represents a certain number of rabbits (on the x axis) and a certain number of foxes (on the y axis).

Since these are the only two variables in the system, each point in this plane describes the complete **state** of the system.

Over time, the state moves around the plane; this figure shows the path traced by the state during the time interval. This path is called a **trajectory**.

Since the behavior of this system is periodic, the resulting trajectory is a loop.

If there are 3 variables in the system, we need 3 dimensions to show the state of the system, so the trajectory is a 3-D curve. You can use `plot3` to trace trajectories in 3 dimensions, but for 4 or more variables, you are on your own.

## 9.7   Glossary

**row vector:** In MATLAB, a matrix that has only one row.

**column vector:** A matrix that has only one column.

**transpose:** An operation that transforms the rows of a matrix into columns (or the other way around, if you prefer).

**system of equations:** A set of equations written in terms of a set of variables such that the equations are intertangled.

**paragraph:** A chunk of code that makes up part of a function, usually with an explanatory comment.

**unpack:** To copy the elements of a vector into a set of variables.

**pack:** To copy values from a set of variables into a vector.

**state:** If a system can be described by a set of variables, the values of those variables are called the state of the system.

**phase plot:** A plot that shows the state of a system as point in the space of possible states.

**trajectory:** A path in a phase plot that shows how the state of a system changes over time.


## 9.8   Exercises

**Exercise 9.2**   *Based on the examples we have seen so far, you would think that all ODEs describe population as a function of time, but that's not true.*

*According to the Wikipedia[1], "The Lorenz attractor, introduced by Edward Lorenz in 1963, is a non-linear three-dimensional deterministic dynamical system derived from the simplified equations of convection rolls arising in the dynamical equations of the atmosphere. For a certain set of parameters the system exhibits chaotic behavior and displays what is today called a strange attractor..."*

*The system is described by this system of differential equations:*

$$x_t = \sigma(y - x) \tag{9.1}$$
$$y_t = x(r - z) - y \tag{9.2}$$
$$z_t = xy - bz \tag{9.3}$$

*Common values for the parameters are $\sigma = 10$, $b = 8/3$ and $r = 28$.*

*Use* `ode45` *to estimate a solution to this system of equations.*

1. *The first step is to write a function named* `lorenz` *that takes* `t` *and* `V` *as input variables, where the components of* `V` *are understood to be the current values of* `x`, `y` *and* `z`. *It should compute the corresponding derivatives and return them in a single column vector.*

2. *The next step is to test your function by calling it from the command line with values like $t = 0$, $x = 1$, $y = 2$ and $z = 3$? Once you get your function working, you should make it a silent function before calling* `ode45`.

3. *Assuming that Step 2 works, you can use* `ode45` *to estimate the solution for the time interval $t_0 = 0$, $t_e = 30$ with the initial condition $x = 1$, $y = 2$ and $z = 3$.*

4. *Use* `plot3` *to plot the trajectory of $x$, $y$ and $z$.*

---

[1]http://en.wikipedia.org/wiki/Lorenz\_attractor

# Chapter 10

# Second-order systems

## 10.1 Nested functions

In the Section 7.1, we saw an example of an M-file with more than one function:

```
function res = duck()
    error = error_func(10)
end

function res = error_func(h)
    rho = 0.3;       % density in g / cm^3
    r = 10;          % radius in cm
    res = ...
end
```

Because the first function ends before the second begins, they are at the same level of indentation. Functions like these are **parallel**, as opposed to **nested**. A nested function is defined inside another, like this:

```
function res = duck()
    error = error_func(10)

    function res = error_func(h)
        rho = 0.3;       % density in g / cm^3
        r = 10;          % radius in cm
        res = ...
    end
end
```

The top-level function, duck, is the **outer function** and error_func is an **inner function**.

Nesting functions is useful because the variables of the outer function can be accessed from the inner function. This is not possible with parallel functions.

In this example, using a nested function makes it possible to move the parameters rho and r out of error_func.

```
function res = duck(rho)
    r = 10;
    error = error_func(10)

    function res = error_func(h)
        res = ...
    end
end
```

Both `rho` and `r` can be accessed from `error_func`. By making `rho` an input argument, we made it easier to test `duck` with different parameter values.

## 10.2   Newtonian motion

Newton's second law of motion is often written like this

$$F = ma$$

where $F$ is the net force acting on a object, $m$ is the mass of the object, and $a$ is the resulting acceleration of the object. In a simple case where the object is moving along a straight line, $F$ and $a$ are scalars, but in general they are vectors.

Even more generally, if $F$ and $a$ vary in time, then they can be thought of as functions that return vectors; that is, $F$ is a function and the result of evaluating $F(t)$ is a vector that describes the net force at time $t$. So a more explicit way to write Newton's law is

$$\forall t : \vec{F}(t) = m\vec{a}(t)$$

The arrangement of this equation suggests that if you know $m$ and $a$ you can compute force, which is true, but in most physical simulations it is the other way around. Based on a physical model, you know $F$ and $m$, and compute $a$.

So if you know acceleration, $a$, as a function of time, how do you find the position of the object, $p$? Well, we know that acceleration is the second derivative of position, so we can write a differential equation

$$p_{tt} = a$$

Where $a$ and $p$ are functions of time that return vectors, and $p_{tt}$ is the second time derivative of $p$.

Because this equation includes a second derivative, it is a second-order ODE. `ode45` can't solve this equation in this form, but by introducing a new variable, $v$, for velocity, we can rewrite it as a system of first-order ODEs.

$$p_t = v$$
$$v_t = a$$

The first equation says that the first derivative of $p$ is $v$; the second says that the derivative of $v$ is $a$.

## 10.3 Freefall

Let's start with a simple example, an object in freefall in a vacuum (where there's no air resistance). Near the surface of the earth, the acceleration of gravity is $g = -9.8 \ m/s^2$, where the minus sign indicates that gravity pulls down.

If the object falls straight down (in the same direction as gravity), we can describe its position with a scalar value, altitude. So this will be a one-dimensional problem, at least for now.

Here is a rate function we can use with ode45 to solve this problem:

```
function res = freefall(t, X)
    p = X(1);       % the first element is position
    v = X(2);       % the second element is velocity

    dpdt = v;
    dvdt = acceleration(t, p, v);

    res = [dpdt; dvdt];     % pack the results in a column vector
end

function res = acceleration(t, p, v)
    g = -9.8;        % acceleration of gravity in m/s^2
    res = g;
end
```

The first function is the rate function. It gets t and X as input variables, where the elements of X are understood to be position and velocity. The return value from freefall is a (column) vector that contains the derivatives of position and velocity, which are velocity and acceleration, respectively.

Computing $p_t$ is easy because we are given velocity as an element of X. The only thing we have to compute is acceleration, which is what the second function does.

acceleration computes acceleration as a function of time, position and velocity. In this example, the net acceleration is a constant, so we don't really have to include all this information yet, but we will soon.

Here's how to run ode45 with this rate function:

```
>> ode45(@freefall, [0, 30], [4000, 0])
```

As always, the first argument is the function handle, the second is the time interval (30 seconds) and the third is the initial condition: in this case, the initial altitude is 4000 meters and the initial velocity is 0. So you can think of the "object" a a skydiver jumping out of an airplane at about 12,000 feet.

Here's what the result looks like:

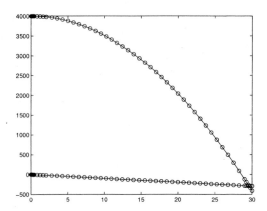

The bottom line shows velocity starting at zero and dropping linearly. The top line shows position starting at 4000 m and dropping parabolically (but remember that this parabola is a function of time, not a ballistic trajectory).

Notice that `ode45` doesn't know where the ground is, so the skydiver keeps going through zero into negative altitude. We will address this issue later.

## 10.4   Air resistance

To make this simulation more realistic, we can add air resistance. For large objects moving quickly through air, the force due to air resistance, called "drag," is proportional to $v^2$:

$$F_{drag} = cv^2$$

Where $c$ is a drag constant that depends on the density of air, the cross-sectional area of the object and the surface properties of the object. For purposes of this problem, let's say that $c = 0.2$.

To convert from force to acceleration, we have to know mass, so let's say that the skydiver (with equipment) weighs 75 kg.

Here's a version of `acceleration` that takes air resistance into account (you don't have to make any changes in `freefall`:

```
function res = acceleration(t, p, v)
    a_grav = -9.8;            % acceleration of gravity in m/s^2
    c = 0.2;                  % drag constant
    m = 75;                   % mass in kg
```

```
    f_drag = c * v^2;          % drag force in N
    a_drag = f_drag / m;       % drag acceleration in m/s^2
    res = a_grav + a_drag;     % total acceleration
end
```

The sign of the drag force (and acceleration) is positive as long as the object is falling, the direction of the drag force is up. The net acceleration is the sum of gravity and drag. Be careful when you are working with forces and accelerations; make sure you only add forces to forces or accelerations to accelerations. In my code, I use comments to remind myself what units the values are in. That helps me avoid nonsense like adding forces to accelerations.

Here's what the result looks like with air resistance:

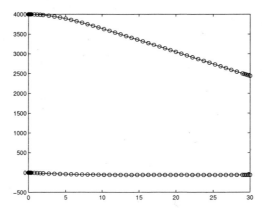

Big difference! With air resistance, velocity increases until the drag acceleration equals $g$; after that, velocity is a constant, known as "terminal velocity," and position decreases linearly (and much more slowly than it would in a vacuum). To examine the results more closely, we can assign them to variables

```
>> [T, M] = ode45(@freefall, [0, 30], [4000, 0]);
```

And then read the terminal position and velocity:

```
>> M(end,1)
```

```
ans = 2.4412e+03          % altitude in meters
```

```
>> M(end,2)
```

```
ans = -60.6143           % velocity in m/s
```

**Exercise 10.1** *Increase the mass of the skydiver, and confirm that terminal velocity increases. This relationship is the source of the intuition that heavy objects fall faster; in air, they do!*

## 10.5   Parachute!

In the previous section, we saw that the terminal velocity of a $75kg$ skydiver is about $60 \ m/s$, which is about 130 mph. If you hit the ground at that speed, you would almost certainly be killed. That's where parachutes come in.

**Exercise 10.2** *Modify* `acceleration` *so that after 30 seconds of free-fall the skydiver deploys a parachute, which (almost) instantly increases the drag constant to 2.7.*

*What is the terminal velocity now? How long (after deployment) does it take to reach the ground?*

## 10.6   Two dimensions

So far we have used `ode45` for a system of first-order equations and for a single second-order equation. The next logical step is a system of second-order equations, and the next logical example is a projectile. A "projectile" is an object propelled through space, usually toward, and often to the detriment of, a target.

If a projectile stays in a plane, we can think of the system as two-dimensional, with $x$ representing the horizontal distance traveled and $y$ representing the height or altitude. So now instead of a skydiver, think of a circus performer being fired out of a cannon.

According to the Wikipedia[1], the record distance for a human cannonball is 65.5 meters (almost 186 feet).

Here is a general framework for computing the trajectory of a projectile in two dimensions using `ode45`:

```
function res = projectile(t, W)
    P = W(1:2);
    V = W(3:4);

    dPdt = V;
    dVdt = acceleration(t, P, V);

    res = [dPdt; dVdt];
end

function res = acceleration(t, P, V)
    g = -9.8;                % acceleration of gravity in m/s^2
    res = [0; g];
end
```

The second argument of the rate function is a vector, `W`, with four elements. The first two are assigned to `P`, which represents position; the last two are assigned to `V`, which represents velocity. `P` and `V` are vectors with elements for the $x$ and $y$ components.

The result from `acceleration` is also a vector; ignoring air resistance (for now), the acceleration in the $x$ direction is 0; in the $y$ direction it's $g$. Other than that, this code is similar to what we saw in Section 10.3.

---

[1]http://en.wikipedia.org/wiki/Human_cannonball

If we launch the human projectile from an initial height of 3 meters, with velocities 40 m/s and 30 m/s in the $x$ and $y$ directions, the `ode45` call looks like this:

```
ode45(@projectile, [0,10], [0, 3, 40, 30]);
```

And the result looks like this:

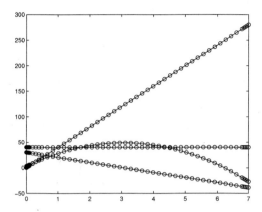

You might have to think a little to figure out which line is which. It looks like the flight time is about 6 seconds.

**Exercise 10.3** *Extract the x and y components of position, plot the trajectory of the projectile, and estimate the distance traveled.*

**Exercise 10.4** *Add air resistance to this simulation. In the skydiver scenario, we estimated that the drag constant was 0.2, but that was based on the assumption that the skydiver is falling flat. A human cannonball, flying head-first, probably has a drag constant closer to 0.1. What initial velocity is needed to achieve the record flight distance of 65.6 meters? Hint: what is the optimal launch angle?*

## 10.7   What could go wrong?

What could go wrong? Well, `vertcat` for one. To explain what that means, I'll start with **catenation**, which is the operation of joining two matrices into a larger matrix. "Vertical catenation" joins the matrices by stacking them on top of each other; "horizontal catenation" lays them side by side.

Here's an example of horizontal catenation with row vectors:

```
>> x = 1:3

x = 1     2     3

>> y = 4:5

y = 4     5
```

```
>> z = [x, y]

z = 1     2     3     4     5
```
Inside brackets, the comma operator performs horizontal catenation. The vertical catenation operator is the semi-colon. Here is an example with matrices:
```
>> X = zeros(2,3)

X =  0     0     0
     0     0     0

>> Y = ones(2,3)

Y =  1     1     1
     1     1     1

>> Z = [X; Y]

Z =  0     0     0
     0     0     0
     1     1     1
     1     1     1
```
These operations only work if the matrices are the same size along the dimension where they are glued together. If not, you get:
```
>> a = 1:3

a = 1     2     3

>> b = a'

b =  1
     2
     3

>> c = [a, b]
??? Error using ==> horzcat
All matrices on a row in the bracketed expression must have the
 same number of rows.

>> c = [a; b]
??? Error using ==> vertcat
All rows in the bracketed expression must have the same
number of columns.
```
In this example, a is a row vector and b is a column vector, so they can't be catenated in either direction.

Reading the error messages, you probably guessed that horzcat is the function that performs horizontal catenation, and likewise with vertcat and vertical catenation.

These operations are relevant to `projectile` because of the last line, which packs `dPdt` and `dVdt` into the output variable:

```
function res = projectile(t, W)
    P = W(1:2);
    V = W(3:4);

    dPdt = V;
    dVdt = acceleration(t, P, V);

    res = [dPdt; dVdt];
end
```

As long as both `dPdt` and `dVdt` are column vectors, the semi-colon performs vertical catenation, and the result is a column vector with four elements. But if either of them is a row vector, that's trouble.

`ode45` expects the result from `projectile` to be a column vector, so if you are working with `ode45`, it is probably a good idea to make *everything* a column vector.

In general, if you run into problems with `horzcat` and `vertcat`, use `size` to display the dimensions of the operands, and make sure you are clear on which way your vectors go.

## 10.8   Glossary

**parallel functions:** Two or more functions defined side-by-side, so that one ends before the next begins.

**nested function:** A function defined inside another function.

**outer function:** A function that contains another function definition.

**inner function:** A function defined inside another function definition. The inner function can access the variables of the outer function.

**catenation:** The operation of joining two matrices end-to-end to form a new matrix.

## 10.9   Exercises

**Exercise 10.5**   *The flight of a baseball is governed by three forces: gravity, drag due to air resistance, and Magnus force due to spin. If we ignore wind and Magnus force, the path of the baseball stays in a plane, so we can model it as a projectile in two dimensions.*

*A simple model of the drag of a baseball is:*

$$F_d = -\frac{1}{2}\, \rho\, v^2\, A\, C_d\, \hat{V}$$

*where $F_d$ is a vector that represents the force on the baseball due to drag, $C_d$ is the drag coefficient (0.3 is a reasonable choice), $\rho$ is the density of air (1.3 kg/m$^3$ at sea level), A is* *the cross sectional area of the baseball ($0.0042\ m^2$), v is the magnitude of the velocity vector, and $\hat{V}$ is a unit vector in the direction of the velocity vector. The mass of the baseball is 0.145 kg.*

*For more information about drag, see http://en.wikipedia.org/wiki/Drag_(physics).*

- *Write a function that takes the initial velocity of the baseball and the launch angle as input variables, uses* **ode45** *to compute the trajectory, and returns the range (horizontal distance in flight) as an output variable.*

- *Write a function that takes the initial velocity of the baseball as an input variable, computes the launch angle that maximizes the range, and returns the optimal angle and range as output variables. How does the optimal angle vary with initial velocity?*

- *When the Red Sox won the World Series in 2007, they played the Colorado Rockies at their home field in Denver, Colorado. Find an estimate of the density of air in the Mile High City. What effect does this have on drag? Make a prediction about what effect this will have on the optimal launch angle, and then use your simulation to test your prediction.*

- *The Green Monster in Fenway Park is about 12 m high and about 97 m from home plate along the left field line. What is the minimum speed a ball must leave the bat in order to clear the monster (assuming it goes off at the optimal angle)? Do you think it is possible for a person to stand on home plate and throw a ball over the Green Monster?*

- *The actual drag on a baseball is more complicated than what is captured by our simple model. In particular, the drag coefficient varies with velocity. You can get some of the details from* The Physics of Baseball[2]; *you also might find information on the web. Either way, specify a more realistic model of drag and modify your program to implement it. How big is the effect on your computed ranges? How big is the effect on the optimal angles?*

---

[2]Robert K. Adair, Harper Paperbacks, 3rd Edition, 2002.

# Chapter 11

# Optimization and Interpolation

## 11.1   ODE Events

Normally when you call `ode45` you have to specify a start time and an end time. But in many cases, you don't know ahead of time when the simulation should end. Fortunately MATLAB provides a mechanism for dealing with this problem. The bad news is that it is a little awkward. Here's how it works:

1. Before calling `ode45` you use `odeset` to create an object called `options` that contains values that control how `ode45` works:

   ```
   options = odeset('Events', @events);
   ```

   In this case, the name of the option is `Events` and the value is a function handle. When `ode45` runs, it will invoke `events` after each timestep. You can call this function anything you want, but the name `events` is conventional.

2. The function you provide has to take the same input variables as your rate function. For example, here is an event function that would work with `projectile` from Section 10.6

   ```
   function [value,isterminal,direction] = events(t,X)
       value = V(2);          % Extract the current height.
       isterminal = 1;        % Stop the integration if height crosses zero.
       direction = -1;        % But only if the height is decreasing.
   end
   ```

   `events` returns three output variables:

   `value` determines when an event occurs. In this case `value` gets the second element of `X`, which is understood to be the height of the projectile. An "event" is a point in time when this value passes through 0.

   `direction` determines whether an event occurs when `value` is increasing (`direction=1`), decreasing (`direction=-1`, or both `direction=0`).

`isterminal` determines what happens when an event occurs. If `isterminal=1`, the event is "terminal" and the simulation stops. If `isterminal=0`, the simulation continues, but `ode45` does some additional work to make sure that the solution in the vicinity of the event is accurate, and that one of the estimated values in the result is at the time of the event.

3. When you call `ode45`, you pass `options` as a fourth argument:

```
ode45(@projectile, [0,10], [0, 3, 40, 30], options);
```

**Exercise 11.1** *How would you modify* `events` *to stop when the height of the projectile falls through 3m?*

## 11.2   Optimization

In Exercise 10.5, you were asked to find the optimal launch angle for a batted ball. "Optimal" is a fancy was of saying "best;" what that means depends on the problem. For the Green Monster Problem—finding the optimal angle for hitting a home run in Fenway Park, the meaning of "optimal" is not obvious.

It is tempting to choose the angle that yields the longest range (distance from home plate when it lands). But in this case we are trying to clear a 12m wall, so maybe we want the angle that yields the longest range when the ball falls through 12m.

Although either definition would be good enough for most purposes, neither is quite right. In this case the "optimal" angle is the one that yields the greatest height at the point where the ball reaches the wall, which is 97m from home plate.

So the first step in any optimization problem is to define what "optimal" means. The second step is to define a range of values where you want to search. In this case the range of feasible values is between 0 degrees (parallel to the ground) and 90 degrees (straight up). We expect the optimal angle to be near 45 degrees, but we might not be sure how far from 45 degrees to look. To play it safe, we could start with the widest feasible range.

The simplest way to search for an optimal value is to run the simulation with a wide range of values and choose the one that yields the best result. This method is not very efficient, especially in a case like this where computing the distance in flight is expensive.

A better algorithm is a Golden Section Search.

## 11.3   Golden section search

To present the Golden Section Search, I will start with a simplified version I'll call a Silver Section Search. The basic idea is similar to the methods for zero-finding we saw in Section 6.5. In the case of zero-finding, we had a picture like this:

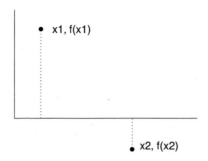

We are given a function, $f$, that we can evaluate, and we want to find a root of $f$; that is, a value of $x$ that makes $f(x) = 0$. If we can find a value, $x_1$, that makes $f(x_1)$ positive and another value, $x_2$, that makes $f(x_2)$ negative, then there has to be a root in between (as long as $f$ is continuous). In this case we say that $x_1$ and $x_2$ "bracket" the root.

The algorithm proceeds by choosing a third value, $x_3$, between $x_1$ and $x_2$ and then evaluating $y = f(x_3)$. If $y$ is positive, we can form a new pair, $(y, x_2)$, that brackets the root. If $y$ is negative then the pair $(x_1, y)$ brackets the root. Either way the size of the bracket gets smaller, so our estimate of the location of the root gets better.

Searching for an optimal value is similar, but we have to start with three values, and the picture looks like this:

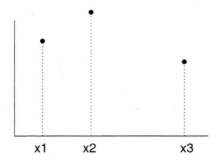

This diagram show that we have evaluated $f$ in three places, $x_1$, $x_2$ and $x_3$, and found that $x_2$ yields the highest value. If $f$ is continuous, then there has to be at least one local maximum between $x_1$ and $x_3$, so we would say that the triple $(x_1, x_2, x_3)$ brackets a maximum.

The next step is to choose a fourth point, $x_4$, and evaluate $f(x_4)$. There are two possible outcomes, depending on whether $f(x_4)$ is greater than $f(x_2)$:

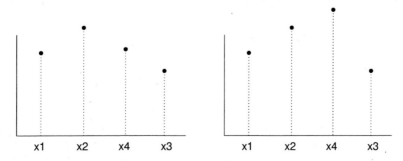

If $f(x_4)$ is less than than $f(x_2)$ (shown on the left), then the new triple $(x_1, x_2, x_4)$ brackets the maximum. If $f(x_4)$ is greater than $f(x_2)$ (shown on the right), then $(x_2, x_4, x_3)$ brackets the maximum. Either way the range gets smaller and our estimate of the optimal value of $x$ gets better.

This method works for almost any value of $x_4$, but some choices are better than others. In the example, I chose to bisect the bigger of the ranges $(x_1, x_2)$ and $(x_2, x_3)$.

Here's what that looks like in MATLAB:

```
function res = optimize(V)
    x1 = V(1);
    x2 = V(2);
    x3 = V(3);

    fx1 = height_func(x1);
    fx2 = height_func(x2);
    fx3 = height_func(x3);

    for i=1:50
        if x3-x2 > x2-x1
            x4 = (x2+x3) / 2;
            fx4 = height_func(x4);
            if fx4 > fx2
                x1 = x2;   fx1 = fx2;
                x2 = x4;   fx2 = fx4;
            else
                x3 = x4;   fx3 = fx4;
            end
        else
            x4 = (x1+x2) / 2;
            fx4 = height_func(x4);
            if fx4 > fx2
                x3 = x2;   fx3 = fx2;
                x2 = x4;   fx2 = fx4;
            else
                x1 = x4;   fx1 = fx4;
            end
        end

        if abs(x3-x1) < 1e-2
            break
        end
    end
    res = [x1 x2 x3];
end
```

The input variable is a vector that contains three values that bracket a maximum; in this case they are angles in degrees. optimize starts by evaluating height_func for each of the three values. We assume that `height_func` returns the quantity we want to optimize; for the Green Monster Problem it is the height of the ball when it reaches the wall.

Each time through the `for` loop the function chooses a value of `x4`, evaluates `height_func`, and then updates the triplet `x1`, `x2` and `x3` according to the results.

After the update, it computes the range of the bracket, `x3-x1`, and checks whether it is small enough. If so, it breaks out of the loop and returns the current triplet as a result. In the worst case the loop executes 50 times.

**Exercise 11.2**  *I call this algorithm a Silver Section Search because it is almost as good as a Golden Section Search. Read the Wikipedia page about the Golden Section Search (http://en.wikipedia.org/wiki/Golden_section_search) and then modify this code to implement it.*

**Exercise 11.3**  *You can write functions that take function handles as input variables, just as* `fzero` *and* `ode45` *do. For example,* `handle_func` *takes a function handle called* `func` *and calls it, passing* `pi` *as an argument.*

```
function res = handle_func(func)
    func(pi)
end
```

*You can call* `handle_func` *from the Command Window and pass different function handles as arguments:*

```
>> handle_func(@sin)

ans = 0

>> handle_func(@cos)

ans = -1
```

*Modify* `optimize` *so that it takes a function handle as an input variable and uses it as the function to be optimized.*

**Exercise 11.4**  *The MATLAB function* `fminsearch` *takes a function handle and searches for a local minimum. Read the documentation for* `fminsearch` *and use it to find the optimal launch angle of a baseball with a given velocity.*

## 11.4   Discrete and continuous maps

When you solve an ODE analytically, the result is a function, which you can think of as a continuous map. When you use an ODE solver, you get two vectors (or a vector and a matrix), which you can think of as a discrete map.

For example, in Section 8.4, we used the following rate function to estimate the population of rats as a function of time:

```
function res = rats(t, y)
    a = 0.01;
    omega = 2 * pi / 365;
    res = a * y * (1 + sin(omega * t));
end
```

The result from ode45 is two vectors:

```
>> [T, Y] = ode45(@rats, [0, 365], 2);
```

T contains the time values where ode45 estimated the population; Y contains the population estimates.

Now suppose we would like to know the population on the 180th day of the year. We could search T for the value 180:

```
>> find(T==180)
```

```
ans = Empty matrix: 0-by-1
```

But there is no guarantee that any particular value appears in T. We can find the index where T crosses 180:

```
>> I = find(T>180); I(1)
```

```
ans = 23
```

I gets the indices of all elements of T greater than 180, so I(1) is the index of the *first* one.

Then we find the corresponding value from Y:

```
>> [T(23), Y(23)]
```

```
ans = 184.3451    40.3742
```

That gives us a coarse estimate of the population on Day 180. If we wanted to do a little better, we could also find the last value before Day 180:

```
>> [T(22), Y(22)]
```

```
ans = 175.2201    36.6973
```

So the population on Day 180 was between 36.6973 and 40.3742.

But where in this range is the best estimate? A simple option is to choose whichever time value is closer to 180 and use the corresponding population estimate. In the example, that's not a great choice because the time value we want is right in the middle.

## 11.5   Interpolation

A better option is to draw a straight line between the two points that bracket Day 180 and use the line to estimate the value in between. This process is called **linear interpolation**, and MATLAB provides a function named **interp1** that does it:

```
>> pop = interp1(T, Y, 180)
```

```
pop = 38.6233
```

The first two arguments specify a discrete map from the values in T to the values in Y. The third argument is the time value where we want to interpolate. The result is what we expected, about halfway between the values that bracket it.

interp1 can also take a fourth argument that specifies what kind of interpolation you want. The default is 'linear', which does linear interpolation. Other choices include 'spline' which uses a spline curve to fit two points on either side, and 'cubic', which uses piecewise cubic Hermite interpolation.

```
>> pop = interp1(T, Y, 180, 'spline')
```

```
pop = 38.6486
```

```
>> pop = interp1(T, Y, 180, 'cubic')
```

```
pop = 38.6491
```

In this case we expect the spline and cubic interpolations to be better than linear, because they use more of the data, and we know the function isn't linear. But we have no reason to expect the spline to be more accurate than the cubic, or the other way around. Fortunately, they are not very different.

We can also use interp1 to project the rat population out beyond the values in T:

```
>> [T(end), Y(end)]
```

```
ans = 365.0000    76.9530
```

```
>> pop = interp1(T, Y, 370, 'cubic')
```

```
pop = 80.9971
```

This process is called **extrapolation**. For time values near 365, extrapolation may be reasonable, but as we go farther into the "future," we expect them to be less accurate. For example, here is the estimate we get by extrapolating for a whole year:

```
>> pop = interp1(T, Y, 365*2, 'cubic')
```

```
pop = -4.8879e+03
```

And that's wrong. So very wrong.

## 11.6   Interpolating the inverse function

We have used interp1 to find population as a function of time; by reversing the roles of T and Y, we can also interpolate time as a function of population. For example, we might want to know how long it takes the population to reach 20.

```
>> interp1(Y, T, 20)
```

```
ans = 133.4128
```

This use of `interp1` might be confusing if you think of the arguments as $x$ and $y$. You might find it helpful to think of them as the range and domain of a map (where the third argument is an element of the range).

The following plot shows $f$ (Y plotted as a function of T) and the inverse of $f$ (T plotted as a function of Y).

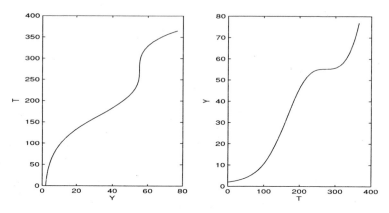

In this case we can use `interp1` either way because $f$ is a **single-valued mapping**, which means that for each value in the domain, there is only one value in the range that maps to it.

If we reduce the food supply so that the rat population decreases during the winter, we might see something like this:

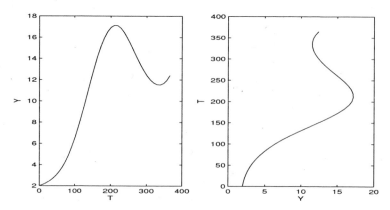

We can still use `interp1` to map from T to Y:

```
>> interp1(T, Y, 260)
```

```
ans = 15.0309
```

So on Day 260, the population is about 15, but if we ask on what day the population was 15, there are two possible answers, 172.44 and 260.44. If we try to use `interp1`, we get the wrong answer:

```
>> interp1(Y, T, 15)
```

```
ans = 196.3833              % WRONG
```

On Day 196, the population is actually 16.8, so `interp1` isn't even close! The problem is that T as a function of Y is a **multivalued mapping**; for some values in the range there are more than one values in the domain. This causes `interp1` to fail. I can't find any documentation for this limitation, so that's pretty bad.

## 11.7   Field mice

As we've seen, one use of interpolation is to interpret the results of a numerical computation; another is to fill in the gaps between discrete measurements.

For example[1], suppose that the population of field mice is governed by this rate equation:

$$g : t, y \rightarrow ay - b(t)y^{1.7}$$

where $t$ is time in months, $y$ is population, $a$ is a parameter that characterizes population growth in the absence of limitations, and $b$ is a function of time that characterizes the effect of the food supply on the death rate.

Although $b$ appears in the equation as a continuous function, we might not know $b(t)$ for all $t$. Instead, we might only have discrete measurements:

| t | b(t) |
|---|------|
| 0 | 0.0070 |
| 1 | 0.0036 |
| 2 | 0.0011 |
| 3 | 0.0001 |
| 4 | 0.0004 |
| 5 | 0.0013 |
| 6 | 0.0028 |
| 7 | 0.0043 |
| 8 | 0.0056 |

If we use **ode45** to solve the differential equation, then we don't get to choose the values of $t$ where the rate function (and therefore $b$) gets evaluated. We need to provide a function that can evaluate $b$ everywhere:

```
function res = interpolate_b(t)
    T = 0:8;
    B = [70 36 11 1 4 13 28 43 56] * 1e-4;
    res = interp1(T, B, t);
end
```

---

[1]This example is adapted from Gerald and Wheatley, *Applied Numerical Analysis*, Fourth Edition, Addison-Wesley, 1989.

Abstractly, this function uses a discrete map to implement a continuous map.

**Exercise 11.5** *Write a rate function that uses* `interpolate_b` *to evaluate g and then use* `ode45` *to compute the population of field mice from t = 0 to t = 8 with an initial population of 100 and a = 0.9.*

*Then modify* `interpolate_b` *to use spline interpolation and run* `ode45` *again to see how much effect the interpolation has on the results.*

## 11.8   Glossary

**interpolation:** Estimating the value of a function using known values on either side.

**extrapolation:** Estimating the value of a function using known values that don't bracket the desired value.

**single-valued mapping:** A mapping where each value in the range maps to a single value in the domain.

**multivalued mapping:** A mapping where at least one value in the range maps to more than one value in the domain.

## 11.9   Exercises

**Exercise 11.6** *A golf ball[2] hit with backspin generates lift, which might increase the range, but the energy that goes into generating spin probably comes at the cost of lower initial velocity. Write a simulation of the flight of a golf ball and use it to find the launch angle and allocation of spin and initial velocity (for a fixed energy budget) that maximizes the horizontal range of the ball in the air.*

*The lift of a spinning ball is due to the Magnus force[3], which is perpendicular to the axis of spin and the path of flight. The coefficient of lift is proportional to the spin rate; for a ball spinning at 3000 rpm it is about 0.1. The coefficient of drag of a golf ball is about 0.2 as long as the ball is moving faster than 20 m/s.*

---

[2]See http://en.wikipedia.org/wiki/Golf_ball.
[3]See http://en.wikipedia.org/wiki/Magnus_effect.

# Chapter 12

# Vectors as vectors

## 12.1 What's a vector?

The word "vector" means different things to different people. In MATLAB, a vector is a matrix that has either one row or one column. So far we have used MATLAB vectors to represent

**sequences:** A sequence is a set of values identified by integer indices; it is natural to store the elements of the sequence as elements of a MATLAB vector.

**state vectors:** A state vector is a set of values that describes the state of a physical system. When you call ode45, you give it in the initial conditions in a state vector. Then when ode45 calls your rate function, it gives you a state vector.

**discrete maps:** If you have two vectors with the same length, you can think of them as a mapping from the elements of one vector to the corresponding elements of the other. For example, in Section 8.5, the results from ode45 are vectors, T and Y, that represent a mapping from the time values in T to the population values in Y.

In this chapter we will see another use of MATLAB vectors: representing spatial vectors. A spatial vector is a value that represents a multidimensional physical quantity like position, velocity, acceleration or force[1].

These quantities cannot be described with a single number because they contain multiple components. For example, in a 3-dimensional Cartesian coordinate space, it takes three numbers to specify a position in space; they are usually called $x$, $y$ and $z$ coordinates. As another example, in 2-dimensional polar coordinates, you can specify a velocity with two numbers, a magnitude and an angle, often called $r$ and $\theta$.

It is convenient to represent spatial vectors using MATLAB vectors because MATLAB knows how to perform most of the vector operations you need for physical modeling. For

---

[1]See http://en.wikipedia.org/wiki/Vector_(spatial).

example, suppose that you are given the velocity of a baseball in the form of a MATLAB vector with two elements, $v_x$ and $v_y$, which are the components of velocity in the $x$ and $y$ directions.

```
>> V = [30, 40]          % velocity in m/s
```

And suppose you are asked to compute the total acceleration of the ball due to drag and gravity. In math notation, the force due to drag is

$$F_d = -\frac{1}{2} \, \rho \, v^2 \, A \, C_d \, \hat{V}$$

where $V$ is a spatial vector representing velocity, $v$ is the magnitude of the velocity (sometimes called "speed"), and $\hat{V}$ is a unit vector in the direction of the velocity vector. The other terms, $\rho$, $A$ and $C_d$, are scalars.

The magnitude of a vector is the square root of the sum of the squares of the elements. You could compute it with **hypotenuse** from Section 5.5, or you could use the MATLAB function **norm** (**norm** is another name[2] for the magnitude of a vector):

```
>> v = norm(V)
```

```
v = 50
```

$\hat{V}$ is a **unit vector**, which means it should have norm 1, and it should point in the same direction as $V$. The simplest way to compute it is to divide $V$ by its own norm.

```
>> Vhat = V / v
```

```
Vhat =   0.6   0.8
```

Then we can confirm that the norm of $\hat{V}$ is 1:

```
>> norm(Vhat)
```

```
ans = 1
```

To compute $F_d$ we just multiply the scalar terms by $\hat{V}$.

```
Fd = - 1/2 * C * rho * A * v^2 * Vhat
```

Similarly, we can compute acceleration by dividing the vector $F_d$ by the scalar $m$.

```
Ad = Fd / m
```

To represent the acceleration of gravity, we create a vector with two components:

```
Ag = [0; -9.8]
```

The $x$ component of gravity is 0; the $y$ component is $-9.8 m/s^2$.

Finally we compute total acceleration by adding vector quantities:

```
A = Ag + Ad;
```

One nice thing about this computation is that we didn't have to think much about the components of the vectors. By treating spatial vectors as basic quantities, we can express complex computations concisely.

---

[2]Magnitude is also called "length" but I will avoid that term because it gets confused with the **length** function, which returns the number of elements in a MATLAB vector.

## 12.2   Dot and cross products

Multiplying a vector by a scalar is a straightforward operation; so is adding two vectors. But multiplying two vectors is more subtle. It turns out that there are two vector operations that resemble multiplication: **dot product** and **cross product**.

The dot product of vectors $A$ and $B$ is a scalar:

$$d = ab \cos \theta$$

where $a$ is the magnitude of $A$, $b$ is the magnitude of $B$, and $\theta$ is the angle between the vectors. We already know how to compute magnitudes, and you could probably figure out how to compute $\theta$, but you don't have to. MATLAB provides a function, `dot`, that computes dot products.

```
d = dot(A, B)
```

`dot` works in any number of dimensions, as long as A and B have the same number of elements.

If one of the operands is a unit vector, you can use the dot product to compute the component of a vector $A$ that is in the direction of a unit vector, $\hat{i}$:

```
s = dot(A, ihat)
```

In this example, $s$ is the **scalar projection** of $A$ onto $\hat{i}$. The **vector projection** is the vector that has magnitude $s$ in the direction of $\hat{i}$:

```
V = dot(A, ihat) * ihat
```

The cross product of vectors $A$ and $B$ is a vector whose direction is perpendicular to $A$ and $B$ and whose magnitude is

$$c = ab \sin \theta$$

where (again) $a$ is the magnitude of $A$, $b$ is the magnitude of $B$, and $\theta$ is the angle between the vectors. MATLAB provides a function, `cross`, that computes cross products.

```
C = cross(A, B)
```

`cross` only works for 3-dimensional vectors; the result is a 3-dimensional vector.

A common use of `cross` is to compute torques. If you represent a moment arm $R$ and a force $F$ as 3-dimensional vectors, then the torque is just

```
Tau = cross(R, F)
```

If the components of R are in meters and the components of F are in Newtons, then the torques in Tau are in Newton-meters.

## 12.3   Celestial mechanics

Modeling celestial mechanics is a good opportunity to compute with spatial vectors. Imagine a star with mass $m_1$ at a point in space described by the vector $P_1$, and a planet with mass $m_2$ at point $P_2$. The magnitude of the gravitational force[3] between them is

---

[3]See http://en.wikipedia.org/wiki/Gravity

$$f_g = G\frac{m_1 m_2}{r^2}$$

where $r$ is the distance between them and $G$ is the universal gravitational constant, which is about $6.67 \times 10^{11} Nm^2/kg^2$. Remember that this is the appropriate value of $G$ only if the masses are in kilograms, distances in meters, and forces in Newtons.

The direction of the force on the star at $P_1$ is in the direction toward $P_2$. We can compute relative direction by subtracting vectors; if we compute R = P2 - P1, then the direction of R is from P1 to P2.

The distance between the planet and star is the length of $R$:

```
r = norm(r)
```

The direction of the force on the star is $\hat{R}$:

```
rhat = R / r
```

**Exercise 12.1**  *Write a sequence of MATLAB statements that computes* F12, *a vector that represents the force on the star due to the planet, and* F21, *the force on the planet due to the star.*

**Exercise 12.2**  *Encapsulate these statements in a function named* gravity_force_func *that takes* P1, m1, P2, *and* m2 *as input variables and returns* F12.

**Exercise 12.3**  *Write a simulation of the orbit of Jupiter around the Sun. The mass of the Sun is about* $2.0 \times 10^{30}$ *kg. You can get the mass of Jupiter, its distance from the Sun and orbital velocity from* http://en.wikipedia.org/wiki/Jupiter. *Confirm that it takes about 4332 days for Jupiter to orbit the Sun.*

## 12.4   Animation

Animation is a useful tool for checking the results of a physical model. If something is wrong, animation can make it obvious. There are two ways to do animation in MATLAB. One is to use getframe to capture a series of images and movie to play them back. The more informal way is to draw a series of plots. Here is an example I wrote for Exercise 12.3:

```
function animate_func(T,M)
    % animate the positions of the planets, assuming that the
    % columns of M are x1, y1, x2, y2.
    X1 = M(:,1);
    Y1 = M(:,2);
    X2 = M(:,3);
    Y2 = M(:,4);

    minmax = [min([X1;X2]), max([X1;X2]), min([Y1;Y2]), max([Y1;Y2])];

    for i=1:length(T)
        clf;
```

```
            axis(minmax);
            hold on;
            draw_func(X1(i), Y1(i), X2(i), Y2(i));
            drawnow;
        end
end
```

The input variables are the output from ode45, a vector T and a matrix M. The columns of M are the positions and velocities of the Sun and Jupiter, so X1 and Y1 get the coordinates of the Sun; X2 and Y2 get the coordinates of Jupiter.

minmax is a vector of four elements which is used inside the loop to set the axes of the figure. This is necessary because otherwise MATLAB scales the figure each time through the loop, so the axes keep changing, which makes the animation hard to watch.

Each time through the loop, animate_func uses clf to clear the figure and axis to reset the axes. hold on makes it possible to put more than one plot onto the same axes (otherwise MATLAB clears the figure each time you call plot).

Each time through the loop, we have to call drawnow so that MATLAB actually displays each plot. Otherwise it waits until you finish drawing all the figures and *then* updates the display.

draw_func is the function that actually makes the plot:

```
function draw_func(x1, y1, x2, y2)
    plot(x1, y1, 'r.', 'MarkerSize', 50);
    plot(x2, y2, 'b.', 'MarkerSize', 20);
end
```

The input variables are the position of the Sun and Jupiter. draw_func uses plot to draw the Sun as a large red marker and Jupiter as a smaller blue one.

**Exercise 12.4** *To make sure you understand how* animate_func *works, try commenting out some of the lines to see what happens.*

One limitation of this kind of animation is that the speed of the animation depends on how fast your computer can generate the plots. Since the results from ode45 are usually not equally spaced in time, your animation might slow down where ode45 takes small time steps and speed up where the time step is larger.

There are two ways to fix this problem:

1. When you call ode45 you can give it a vector of points in time where it should generate estimates. Here is an example:

```
end_time = 1000;
step = end_time/200;
[T, M] = ode45(@rate_func, [0:step:end_time], W);
```

The second argument is a range vector that goes from 0 to 1000 with a step size determined by step. Since step is end_time/200, there will be about 200 rows in T and M (201 to be precise).

This option does not affect the accuracy of the results; ode45 still uses variable time steps to generate the estimates, but then it interpolates them before returning the results.

2. You can use pause to play the animation in real time. After drawing each frame and calling drawnow, you can compute the time until the next frame and use pause to wait:

```
dt = T(i+1) - T(i);
pause(dt);
```

A limitation of this method is that it ignores the time required to draw the figure, so it tends to run slow, especially if the figure is complex or the time step is small.

**Exercise 12.5** *Use* animate_func *and* draw_func *to vizualize your simulation of Jupiter. Modify it so it shows one day of simulated time in 0.001 seconds of real time—one revolution should take about 4.3 seconds.*

## 12.5   Conservation of Energy

A useful way to check the accuracy of an ODE solver is to see whether it conserves energy. For planetary motion, it turns out that ode45 does not.

The kinetic energy of a moving body is $mv^2/2$; the kinetic energy of a solar system is the total kinetic energy of the planets and sun. The potential energy of a sun with mass $m_1$ and a planet with mass $m_2$ and a distance $r$ between them is

$$U = -G\frac{m_1 m_2}{r}$$

**Exercise 12.6** *Write a function called* energy_func *that takes the output of your Jupiter simulation,* T *and* M, *and computes the total energy (kinetic and potential) of the system for each estimated position and velocity. Plot the result as a function of time and confirm that it decreases over the course of the simulation. Your function should also compute the relative change in energy, the difference between the energy at the beginning and end, as a percentage of the starting energy.*

You can reduce the rate of energy loss by decreasing ode45's tolerance option using odeset (see Section 11.1):

```
options = odeset('RelTol', 1e-5);
[T, M] = ode45(@rate_func, [0:step:end_time], W, options);
```

The name of the option is RelTol for "relative tolerance." The default value is 1e-3 or 0.001. Smaller values make ode45 less "tolerant," so it does more work to make the errors smaller.

**Exercise 12.7** *Run* ode45 *with a range of values for* RelTol *and confirm that as the tolerance gets smaller, the rate of energy loss decreases.*

**Exercise 12.8** *Run your simulation with one of the other ODE solvers MATLAB provides and see if any of them conserve energy.*

## 12.6   What is a model for?

In Section 7.2 I defined a "model" as a simplified description of a physical system, and said that a good model lends itself to analysis and simulation, and makes predictions that are good enough for the intended purpose.

Since then, we have seen a number of examples; now we can say more about what models are for. The goals of a model tend to fall into three categories.

**prediction:** Some models make predictions about physical systems. As a simple example, the duck model in Exercise 6.2 predicts the level a duck floats at. At the other end of the spectrum, global climate models try to predict the weather tens or hundreds of years in the future.

**design:** Models are useful for engineering design, especially for testing the feasibility of a design and for optimization. For example, in Exercise 11.6 you were asked to design the golf swing with the perfect combination of launch angle, velocity and spin.

**explanation:** Models can answer scientific questions. For example, the Lotka-Volterra model in Section 9.4 offers a possible explanation of the dynamics of animal populations systems in terms of interactions between predator and prey species.

The exercises at the end of this chapter include one model of each type.

## 12.7   Glossary

**spatial vector:** A value that represents a multidimensional physical quantity like position, velocity, acceleration or force.

**norm:** The magnitude of a vector. Sometimes called "length," but not to be confused with the number of elements in a MATLAB vector.

**unit vector:** A vector with norm 1, used to indicate direction.

**dot product:** A scalar product of two vectors, proportional to the norms of the vectors and the cosine of the angle between them.

**cross product:** A vector product of two vectors with norm proportional to the norms of the vectors and the sine of the angle between them, and direction perpendicular to both.

**projection:** The component of one vector that is in the direction of the other (might be used to mean "scalar projection" or "vector projection").

## 12.8   Exercises

**Exercise 12.9**  *If you put two identical bowls of water into a freezer, one at room temperature and one boiling, which one freezes first?*

*Hint: you might want to do some research on the Mpemba effect.*

**Exercise 12.10**  *You have been asked to design a new skateboard ramp; unlike a typical skateboard ramp, this one is free to pivot about a support point. Skateboarders approach the ramp on a flat surface and then coast up the ramp; they are not allowed to put their feet down while on the ramp. If they go fast enough, the ramp will rotate and they will gracefully ride down the rotating ramp. Technical and artistic display will be assessed by the usual panel of talented judges.*

*Your job is to design a ramp that will allow a rider to accomplish this feat, and to create a physical model of the system, a simulation that computes the behavior of a rider on the ramp, and an animation of the result.*

**Exercise 12.11**  *A binary star system contains two stars orbiting each other and sometimes planets that orbit one or both stars[4]. In a binary system, some orbits are "stable" in the sense that a planet can stay in orbit without crashing into one of the stars or flying off into space.*

*Simulation is a useful tool for investigating the nature of these orbits, as in Holman, M.J. and P.A. Wiegert, 1999, "Long-Term Stability of Planets in Binary Systems," Astronomical Journal 117, available from* http://citeseer.ist.psu.edu/358720.html.

*Read this paper and then modify your planetary simulation to replicate or extend the results.*

---

[4]See http://en.wikipedia.org/wiki/Binary_star.